D1431755

CHAIN SAW MANUAL

R. P. SARNA

Division Forester
American Pulpwood Association

CHAIN SAW

REEDSBURG PUBLIC LIBRARY
345 VINE STREET
REEDSBURG, WI 53959

MANUAL

Order from **IPP**

THE INTERSTATE
Printers & Publishers, Inc.

DANVILLE, ILLINOIS 61832

REEDSBURG PUBLIC LIBRARY
345 VINE STREET
REEDSBURG, WI 53959

CHAIN SAW MANUAL
Modified Edition

Copyright © 1980 by the American Pulpwood Association. First Edition, 1979. All rights reserved. Published by The Interstate Printers & Publishers, Inc., Danville, Illinois. Printed in the United States of America.

Library of Congress Card No. 80-50311

ISBN 0-8134-2133-0

PREFACE

This book is designed to serve as a guide for classroom use and to help the homeowner use his chain saw somewhat more safely. Although we would like to write a how-to-do-it book that would make each reader an expert in the use of a chain saw, we can't because experience, as in many other endeavors, is necessary.

Forests vary widely in timber size, density, climate, and in other conditions. The techniques suggested in this book will enable the logger to put a tree safely on the ground anywhere in the world. However, loggers in some areas of the world use other techniques that may be more suited to their conditions. Cutters in those areas should probably learn these other techniques as well.

To be a skilled logger, you must continue learning. This book will be a worthy start—but just a start—of your education.

ACKNOWLEDGEMENTS

Although thanking all the people involved in the preparation of this book is difficult, I would be remiss if I failed to publicly state my indebtedness to a few of them.

Thanks to Dick Borgnis, who taught me the basics of logging and that silviculturally and aesthetically sound logging operations can be commercially successful, and thanks to Dr. Tom Corcoran, who taught me to see that all parts of a logging operation are not just parts but phases of a larger system.

A special thanks to Lars Varland, who taught me how much I didn't know and who inspired the idea for this book. Lars, in his travels and demonstrations around the world for Husqvarna picked up many new ideas and subtleties of technique, and after seeing his demonstrations, I believed that a book had to be written which would give at least a basic approach to the use of the chain saw, specifically for new people starting out in the woods.

Thanks should also be given to Herb Flint and his colleagues at the Emergency Medical Services Project, Medical Care Development, Inc., in Augusta, Maine, for their assistance in the preparation of Chapter 8, "Medical Help After Injuries."

Thanks are also due to the many members of the Safety and Training Committee of the Northeastern Technical Division of the American Pulpwood Association for their review of and comments on the text, and to Art Wimble, Administrative Assistant, American Pulpwood Association, Washington, D.C., for his review of the text and for his efforts in seeing it through to publication.

And, finally, thanks to all the many dealers, distributors, and manufacturers who provided information and photographs.

CONTENTS

CHAPTER 1

Saws and Accessories

Like the recipe for rabbit stew that begins with the acquisition of a rabbit, before you can use a chain saw, you have to have one. The choice of the chain saw can affect the health, production, and finances of its user.

A potential chain saw purchaser must first find out about the dealers in his area. The dealer's most important stock in trade is not the saws he sells but his service. The best saw in the world can be rendered useless for want of a small part, and the dealer who cannot supply that part, along with speedy service, will cost the professional logger a great deal of idle time during which he will not be earning any wages. A dealer may carry several brands of saws. The availability of parts for the different brands may vary, so it is wise to choose a dealer with a good reputation and then consider his advice carefully when you are choosing the saw.

Engine Size

Over the years many wild claims have been made about the horsepower of various saws. Like Detroit automobiles, horsepower is determined by testing stripped down engines at impractical speeds and then seasoning these readings heavily with salesmen's imaginations. The actual horsepower produced by various brands of saws is approximately equal for engines of about the same displacement. The table of horsepower output for various saws as tested in Sweden by an independent laboratory will be surprising to many salesmen.

1

Some Representative Saw Horsepowers
As Tested in Sweden

Saw*	Displacement	RPM	HP
Brand A	3.5	8,400	3.2
Brand B	2.5	8,800	2.6
Brand C	3.8	9,000	3.8
Brand D	4.7	8,700	4.5
Brand E	3.8	7,500	3.0
Brand F	3.3	8,500	3.2
Brand G	2.9	8,000	3.2

*Some saws are sold in Scandinavia.

Knowing the horsepower of his saw doesn't really help a logger. Since the power output of saws of equal displacement is roughly about the same, most saws are chosen by their displacement and can be roughly grouped into four categories. The first is the "mini-saws," the ¼-inch-pitch chain saws which are designed

Fig. 1—This McCulloch is a good example of a mini-saw used mostly by homeowners and casual users. Note, however, a chain brake is available.

primarily for homeowners, although they are sometimes used in mills for trimming lumber and for other jobs. In general, they are not designed for continuous production use.

The next size saw is an in-between size. Some of these saws are actually designed to be used full time by professional loggers. On occasion they are used in combination with a larger saw, the larger saw being used for felling and bucking and the smaller saw for limbing. Their engines are roughly in the 2.5-cubic-inch or 40-cc. displacement category, and they use either a ⅜-inch-pitch chain or .325-inch-pitch chain, which is slightly smaller. There is

Fig. 2—A medium-sized pulpwood saw, this one is a McCulloch ProMac 55 with a chain brake.

some overlap here between the larger saws meant for the occasional user and the smaller saws used by professional loggers. The professional saw generally has an engine built for continuous use, a good muffler, vibration isolation, etc.; and, as a result, it generally costs quite a bit more than the saw built to be sold in the city hardware store.

The third category of saw could be called the lightweight professional saw. This is by far the most popular saw in use by professional loggers. These saws run ⅜-inch-pitch chain and can be put into three classes according to engine size. The 3½-cubic-inch saw is definitely a small pulpwood saw. The 4-cubic-inch size is a good all-around saw for both pulp and small softwood timber. The 5-cubic-inch size is the most common saw for the saw timber of the Northeast.

In Maine, for instance, a 1974 survey of chain saws by the State Department of Manpower Affairs suggests that about 46 percent of the saws in that state were of one brand. Out of those, about half were 3.5-cubic-inch saws and about half 4-cubic-inch saws. Generally, as the trees get larger so do the saws. In the larger hardwoods of southern New England, the 5-cubic-inch-size saw is much more prevalent.

Fig. 3—A good example of a northeastern logger's saw, a Jonsereds 70.

Fig. 4—A Partner P100, a large, powerful "West Coast–type" saw.

The fourth category of saws can be termed the heavy professional models. They are often referred to as "West Coast saws" because they are a common size of saw in that area. They generally have 6 cubic inches of displacement or more and run .404-inch-pitch chain. It is not uncommon to see this type of saw used in the Northeast by tree crews in felling large hardwoods, in felling large roadside trees, and often in bucking on landings where the larger chain and greater power sometimes give this type of saw an advantage in bucking dirty wood.

Chain Size

By far the most popular chain size in the Northeast is the ⅜-inch pitch. It is fast cutting, the square-cornered chisel types especially so, and it gives good service life if properly maintained. The smaller sizes of chain, because of their narrower kerf, more efficiently use the engine power and cut faster on small sizes of wood. However, they do not have the chip-carrying capacity of the larger chains; therefore, they are not as effective on long bars. Since the cutters are smaller, they cannot be sharpened as many times as the larger chain. Generally, a ¼-inch-pitch chain is for the

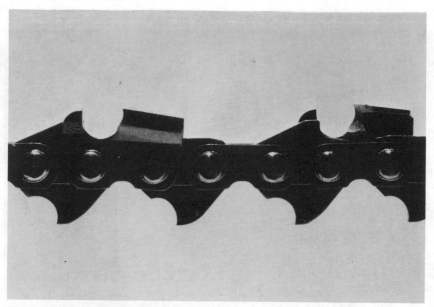

Fig. 5—The latest types of chains have chisel-shaped (sharp square-cornered) cutters and some type of ramp-like projections to keep objects from getting caught in front of the depth gauges. These new types of chains cut faster, hold their edge better, and have somewhat less tendency to kick back.

occasional user who does not consider chain life to be an important factor. In addition, the mini-sized engine does not have the power to pull the larger-sized chains. An exception might be the .325-inch-pitch chain which is designed for the smaller professional saws. Chains such as the .404 size and even larger are used for cutting very large wood where the ability to carry the chips out of a long cut is a problem and on larger displacement and gear-drive saws where the actual physical breaking strength of the chain may be important.

Chains also come in various "gauges." The gauge is the thickness of the drive-link tang, the little bump that comes down from the bottom of the chain. This drive tang slides along the groove in the bar to guide the chain. Obviously, the gauge of the chain must be the proper size to fit the groove in the bar—this is one of several instances in which your dealer's knowledge (and his reference books!) will be very important to you.

In general, most manufacturers stick to one or two gauges for their lines. Homelite and Stihl use .050 gauge for their ⅜-inch-pitch chain and .063 gauge for their .404-inch-pitch chain. McCulloch uses .058 throughout. All Scandinavian saws use .058 gauge, and most of them have interchangeable bars and chains. However, when they are sold in this country, the importers sometimes change bars and chains. Husqvarna, for example, in this country uses Oregon bars that were designed to fit the Homelite XL12 and 900 Series saws; and, therefore, the Husqvarna saws in the United States use .050-gauge chain, while Husqvarna saws in Canada use .058. Again, it is important that you use the right gauge chain for your bar. If you have a .058 bar, for example, and try to use a .050-gauge chain, the chain will wobble in the groove and wear the bar rapidly, as well as not cut properly. Of course, if you try to use .063-gauge chain on a new bar, it will not fit, or if you try to use it on a badly worn bar, it might fit but it will be too tight to run properly.

Bar Length

The length of the guide bar, of course, varies with the size of the trees that are generally being cut. While it is possible to fell a tree of a diameter slightly over twice the usable length of the guide bar, in practice, if a logger had to do this for every tree, it would slow down his production tremendously. On the other hand, not only are long bars more expensive, but the logger also is more apt to stick the tip of the bar down into some place he can't see, thus resulting in a kickback* accident and perhaps a serious injury. In general, most loggers use a guide bar that has a length as great as the diameter of most of the trees they are cutting. An occasional larger tree is not that much more of a problem. Most pulpwood loggers use about a 16-inch bar. In saw timber areas, with the larger tree size, the 18-inch and 20-inch sizes are more popular, and, of course, in certain areas, 24-inch or larger bars may be needed.

Chain Tension

For maximum chain life, the chain should be properly tensioned. This has always been difficult with solid-nosed bars be-

---

*Kickback refers to the action of the chain catching on something, which causes the saw to be thrown back violently, often causing serious injury. Kickback will be explained in greater detail in Chapter 3 and Chapter 5.

cause the chain develops a great deal of heat from friction as it slides over the nose of the bar. The heat causes the chain to expand and hence become too slack. If the chain is properly tensioned when cold, it will be too slack when running. If the chain is tensioned after it warms up, then stopping the saw long enough to refuel it might result in the chain shrinking to the bar so tight that it will not turn.

The first attempt at solving these problems was the roller-nosed bar. This bar cuts down on the friction considerably but is somewhat fragile, and since the chain is unsupported during part of its travel, it is not good practice to cut with the tip of the bar. The sprocket-nosed bar seems to have solved these problems. Here a thin sheet metal sprocket, roughly the thickness of the drive links, is all but hidden inside the nose of the bar. As the chain approaches the end of the bar, the sprocket lifts the drive link and therefore keeps the saw from running on the rails of the bar as it travels around the nose. This cuts friction considerably, and yet the chain is still supported well enough that the nose of the bar may be used in cutting. It is true that a saw with a sprocket-nosed bar will kick harder, as there is so little friction between the chain and the bar, and the sprocket nose may be somewhat more fragile, particularly if it is pinched in a cut. On the other hand, its advantages often outweigh its disadvantages. It gives faster cutting, better chain life, and better chain tension, which in itself is a safety factor. Most sprockets and bearings for bars can be replaced by a dealer, although if the nose portion of the bar is bent, the bar is ruined. Some sprocket-nosed bars are available with the entire tip of the bar made as a section that may easily be replaced by the user.

Sprocket Selection

Most loggers realize that most saws can be fitted with a wide variety of chain sizes and bar lengths. The drive sprocket can also be changed. There are two general types of sprockets. One is the spur-type sprocket which looks like a star cut out of a sheet of metal about ½ inch thick. In direct drive saws, the spur-type is generally fastened permanently to the clutch drum. The rim-type sprocket consists of a clutch drum with a splined shaft and a small ring that slides over the splined shaft. The ring has small pockets cut into its circumference, each pocket slightly wider than the gauge of the chain and shaped like a drive link. As the sprockets wear, they can be replaced with either type. With the spur-type sprocket, the sprocket and drum assembly is replaced; whereas, with the rim type, usually just the rim is replaced. Generally, both type sprockets with various numbers of teeth are available. For example, with a ⅜-inch-pitch chain, many saws will take either a seven- or an eight-tooth sprocket. The eight-tooth sprocket is popular in Scandinavia. The larger number of teeth gives greater chain speed, which is somewhat of a help in limbing technique on small branches. The seven-tooth sprocket, however, may produce faster cutting, particularly with larger logs. The eight-tooth sprocket and higher chain speed do require a lighter touch on the saw, which may be advantageous. If you "bear down" on your saw out of habit, then you will probably require the seven-tooth sprocket; and if you use a long bar, you almost certainly will require it. Kickback is also related to a certain range of chain speed.

Other Saw Features

The imported saws have increased in popularity tremendously in the last few years partly because of their many features which American saws did not have at that time. Now, many American saws have these features too, and they are well worth considering.

Anti-vibration Mountings

Both the moving parts in the engine and the action of the chain as it cuts through wood produce vibration. This vibration is fatiguing to the user and may cause other health problems. Reynaud's or Traumatic Vasospastic Disease is a malfunction of the circulation in the hands and/or feet. Although heredity evidently plays a large part in its cause, it apparently is aggravated by vibration, cold, and nicotine. Anyone troubled with this disease should most certainly investigate saws with vibration isolation. The lessened fatigue from vibration makes these saws attractive to most loggers. Since the greater the mass, the more the damping effect; theoretically, those saws which have the handlebars and fuel tank as a unit separated from the other parts of the saw

Fig. 6—Rubber vibration isolation elements cut down on the vibration transmitted to the handlebars of the saw and make the saw less fatiguing to use. Note, however, on this older, well-used saw that the handlebars have been bent and the block is misaligned. This can reduce the damping qualities considerably.

dampen the vibration the most. In practice, however, there are many other factors which influence the effectiveness of a vibration isolation system. For instance, the composition of the rubber elements is important. Many saw manufacturers provide rubber mounts of different compositions, since with a long bar the softer mounts are compressed too easily. The stiffer rubber mounts are not necessary on a shorter bar, however, and would not stop as much vibration from reaching the user's hands.

Muffler

An effective muffler is extremely important. The effective horsepower added by a noisy muffler or the elimination of a muffler is, contrary to popular misconception, insignificant. The prevalent misconception that it is impossible to muffle a two-cycle engine without harming it is also completely wrong. There is a limit, however, as to how effective a muffler can be and still be small enough to fit on a chain saw. Besides, the fan and chain also contribute a great deal of noise. Unfortunately, hearing loss occurs gradually, and by the time it has progressed enough that you are aware of it, it is too late. Since hearing loss cannot be restored, for your own health, get a saw with a quiet muffler. Some saws are available with extra quiet mufflers at a slight additional cost, and most saws manufactured or sold (as some American saws are) in Scandinavian countries have fairly quiet mufflers. In addition, however, the logger should consider breaking with tradition and wear ear protection. In the winter, earmuff-type hearing protectors not only cut out noise but also keep the ears warm. In the summer, ear plugs or the special "Swedish Wool" will protect the hearing without being hot and uncomfortable.

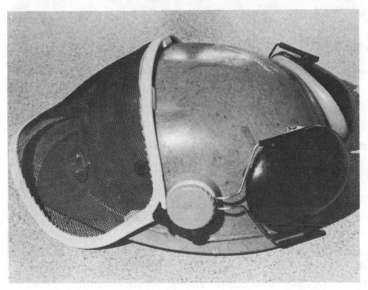

Fig. 7—A hard hat with face protection screen and ear muffs for noise protection. The face screen is quite popular in Scandinavian countries.

Upon exposure to loud noise, the hearing "threshold" shifts, so that your hearing is automatically, temporarily turned "down." After you have been running a noisy chain saw for a few minutes, your threshold will shift, and you won't be able to hear as well as you could before you started the saw. You then will not think the saw is so noisy—whereas, you actually cannot hear as well for a while. Hearing protection can help prevent this.

Fig. 8—Many types of ear plug material are available. This is "Swedish Wool." Make sure you follow the directions on the package for using the plugs exactly.

Chain Brake

Cuts from the moving chain cause most of the accidental injuries in the woods. Many of these are caused by kickback, which occurs when the saw chain catches on something and the saw bar is thrown back so quickly that your reaction time is too slow to stop it from causing an injury. (The cause of and the preventive measures for kickback are discussed in greater detail in Chapter 3.) This is an instance in which the chain brake becomes an important safety device. The chain brake is a mechanism that will stop the chain in a very small fraction of a second when the device is triggered by pressure on a lever that is placed before the front handlebar. If the saw is thrown back violently or if the user's hand slips off the handlebar and hits the lever, the chain stops before injury can occur. The most common type of chain brake is a spring-band brake applied around the clutch drum by a spring, triggered by the lever. Homelite, McCulloch, Husqvarna, Partner, and JoBu use this type. Jonsereds uses a shoe-type brake against the clutch drum and in some cases an ignition cut off as well. Stihl uses an extra clutch in addition to the brake to stop the chain. Any chain brake, with the exception of the type which shuts off the ignition, can be used to start the saw without the chain moving; to pass a running saw up in a tree to someone, as in the case of tree surgery work; and, with the engine shut off, to hold the chain when you are sharpening the saw. Considering the cost of medical attention, a chain brake is an excellent investment for its safety value alone.

Electronic Ignition

Chain saws have generally used a magneto built into the flywheel to provide ignition voltage. Up until a few years ago, a set of breaker points like those in an automobile were necessary as part of the system. The contact points became burned and pitted, and the movement of the fiber block on the cam wore the block down and changed the point gap and, hence, the timing. So, it was

Fig. 9—An electronic or capacitor discharge ignition system has no moving parts to wear out. All the electronic elements are sealed inside a block of epoxy, where moisture and dirt cannot get at them.

necessary periodically to change the points and condenser. This was not a major task, but it did result in down time for the saw; furthermore, during part of the time that the saw was running, the ignition system would not be quite perfect. Generally, it would get harder and harder to start or it would overheat, and then it would finally have to be taken in to have the points replaced. Dampness might also get to the points and prevent the saw from starting. This was particularly true if a cold saw was taken into a warm building during the winter. The condensation that formed inside might raise havoc with the points. (It is better to leave the saw outside all the time.)

A good electronic ignition system eliminates all these problems. By means of transistor-like devices, all moving parts are eliminated. Various manufacturers over the years have produced electronic ignition systems with varying degrees of success. The first ones certainly had more than their share of troubles. In the last few years, however, electronic ignition systems have progressed to the point where they are about as trouble-free as a

Fig. 10—Bucking spikes help to control the saw in many types of cutting.

transistor radio. In fact, many manufacturers now give lifetime guarantees. Although electronic ignition adds to the purchase price of the saw, you will save on down time and maintenance costs, and when that misty day comes when your saw will start while no one else's will, you'll be glad you have it.

There are various other features that come on saws these days, and doubtless the manufacturers are devising many more that they haven't told us about yet. Some of these features are standard, and some are optional. Some features, such as devices to guard the user's hand in case the chain should break, just sit there quietly waiting for the chance to protect you. A broken chain is an extremely rare occurrence if you maintain the chain properly, but it's important to have this type of guard just in case. Also helpful is a little metal finger underneath the bottom of the saw to help catch the chain if it should break. Most professional saws have a device to hold the throttle partly open when you start the saw. Not only is this a handy feature, but it's also a safety feature, since it frees one

Fig. 11—A "whip" attached to a saw can be adjusted so that the saw can be used for measuring 4-foot lengths of pulpwood.

hand and keeps the user from wishing he had an extra hand in order to get the saw started. Most saws sold overseas also have an extra little trigger on the top outside the rear handle. The purpose of this device is to prevent the throttle from being opened accidentally when the user's hand isn't on the saw. This could happen when the saw is being carried through brush. This is a good device, and since most of the recent ones are trouble-free, it's hard to find an excuse for those loggers who tape it down. An optional feature that is popular in some areas is a handlebar heating system which uses a small bit of hot exhaust gas tapped from the muffler and piped to the inside of the handle, or to a generator and electrically heated handle, which makes the saw more comfortable to use in the winter but which can be turned off during the summer months. Some loggers may find this a pleasing accessory. Others troubled with circulation diseases in their hands may find it a necessity.

CHAPTER 2

Saw Maintenance

It is unfortunate that many loggers don't realize that the maintenance of their saws has a major effect on productivity. Some men wear out several saws a year and are always having trouble with their saws. Other men's saws just seem to keep on working forever. One of the major differences is in the maintenance that the saws receive. Actually, proper maintenance takes very little time. Proper maintenance means *preventative* maintenance. If something breaks or wears out prematurely, then it's going to take much more time to fix your saw and that's time during which you could have been cutting wood. The key to long saw life is spending just a little time now and then to take care of your saw so that major troubles don't occur later.

Fuel Mix

All present-day saws are powered by what an engineer would call a two-stroke-cycle, crankcase-scavanged gasoline engine. In the crankcase-scavanged engine, the piston comes down on a power stroke, traps the fuel-air mixture in the crankcase and compresses it. This fuel-air mixture under pressure is squirted up on top the piston to blow the exhaust gases out and to fill the combustion chamber with the mixture that will be burned on the next power stroke. This method of operation results in an engine that is very light for its power output. However, it also results in two disadvantages: First, the engine cannot have a crankcase filled with oil for lubrication like most engines do, since all the oil

would be blown up into the cyclinder. This means that the lubricating oil must be mixed in with the gasoline. Second, because the
oil is mixed with the gasoline, there is a limit to the compression
ratio that can be used, since lubricating oil has a very low octane
rating and a mixture of oil and gas therefore averages out to a fairly
low octane rating. Consequently, the fuel used, the oil used, and
the mixture of the two have an important effect on the operation
and life of the engine.

All saws are made to operate on regular gasoline. High octane
gasoline (made from regular gasoline with the addition of tetraethyl lead) is unnecessary and may result in lead deposits building up inside the combustion chamber. Some "no lead" gasolines
which have had phosphate compounds added to take the place of
the tetraethyl lead may cause problems with the lubricating oil.
All in all, a regular leaded gasoline is your best bet.

The most important thing you can do for the fuel is to keep it
clean. To comply with safety regulations, you should store your
fuel in a labeled metal can. Many loggers keep their fuel in old
10-quart or 5-gallon oil cans. If properly labeled, they probably
meet the safety requirements in most states. However, most oil
cans have a flat top with a beaded rim that joins the sides of the
can to the top. As a result, all kinds of dirt, dust, hay, grass, wood
chips, water, snow, and other debris accumulate on the top of the
can. When you fuel up your saw, some of this garbage falls in the
tank. In the summer, you'll wonder why the fuel filter in your saw
clogs up so fast. In the winter, you'll wonder why there is ice in
the fuel line. Flat-top cans turn out to be a false economy in the
long run. There are some 5-gallon oil cans with round-domed tops
and spouts which may prove satisfactory if properly labeled. Metal
safety cans made of heavy gauge metal with wire screens and
spring-loaded tops seem like a good idea. However, many of the
models now available spray gas in such a large stream from their
spouts that it is impossible to add fuel to your saw without spilling
gasoline all over it, thus creating a fire hazard. Cans with funnels
which obscure a clear view into the tank can result in overfilling
the saw with the same result. Two and one-half to 5-gallon
gasoline cans of the type sold to homeowners to fuel lawn mowers
have proven satisfactory in many areas.

There have been many advances in lubricating oils in the last
few years. Certainly, detergent oils have proven themselves in all
heavy-duty applications. Your saw will also benefit from a deter-

gent oil. However, do *not* under any circumstance use the kind of detergent oil that you would use in a car or a bulldozer. The detergent additives in those oils when burned result in a hard metallic ash. The oil that you put in your chain saw will eventually be burned in the combustion chamber. If metal deposits form on the cylinder and on the exhaust ports, this sharp, hard metallic ash can cut the rings and piston on your saw as effectively as a handful of sand thrown into the engine. On the other hand, don't use non-detergent automobile engine oil either. It doesn't give the engine the protection it deserves and may not mix well with the gasoline. The few cents more per quart for proper two-cycle engine oil will pay dividends in the long run.

Different brands of saws require different fuel-oil mixtures. Some saws require 1 part of oil to 16 parts of gasoline, some 1 part oil to 20 parts gasoline, some 1 part oil to 25 parts gasoline, and some 1 part oil to 40 parts gasoline. It is important that you refer to the instruction manual that came with your saw, or, if you have lost that, consult your dealer. Too little oil will result in too little lubrication of the engine, resulting in high wear. Too much oil is not needed for lubrication and will result in carbon deposits in the combustion chamber, on the piston, and in the muffler, and in a lowering of the octane rating of the fuel-oil mix. Unfortunately, people with good intentions sometimes have both these problems. These problems are brought on by not mixing the fuel and oil thoroughly; consequently, the oil later settles out of the gasoline, resulting in the first tankful of gasoline having very little oil and the last tankful from the fuel can having too much oil. Make it a practice to mix your fuel thoroughly, and make it a habit to always swirl or shake your fuel can before you add fuel to the saw.

Some loggers also have a problem getting the proper ratios. On an operation with many cutters, it may pay to mix the fuel up in large batches. Put some gasoline in first, add the oil, then the rest of the gasoline, making sure they are mixed thoroughly and stirring occasionally with a clean wooden paddle. After the fuel cans have been filled and have been taken back into the woods, they still should be shaken or swirled each time before gas is added to the saw.

Chain Oil

Far too many loggers use motor oil to lubricate their bars and chains. The chains on most saws today travel at a high speed and quickly throw off motor oil from the chain. Consequently, the motor oil is wasted because it isn't on the chain long enough to do much good. The oil made by oil companies specifically for the lubrication of saw chain costs much more to buy. However, it has been proven the chain will last many times longer, and the savings on the chain will more than make up for the extra cost of the oil. Bar and chain oil is "sticky," so that much less of it is thrown off; therefore, it stays on the chain and does its job. If for some reason you are unable to buy bar and chain oil in your area, buy SAE #80 Gear Lube. This is quite similar to the bar and chain oil but will probably cost you slightly more.

Many of the bar and chain oils packaged by the oil companies are now multiple viscosity. They don't thicken up quite so fast in the winter. However, even these will become too thick in extremely cold weather. Thick, cold oil of any type will raise havoc with the automatic oiler on your saw. Because the automatic oiler is expensive to replace, when it's very cold, thin the oil somewhat with a little bit of kerosene or diesel fuel.

Again, don't use old flat-top oil cans to store your bar and chain oil. The dirt that collects on top is just as bad when it passes through the oil pump of your saw. Most automatic oilers have a small piston that fits very closely in a little cylinder. A small amount of grit here will cause another big repair bill. Plastic bleach jugs thoroughly cleaned out and properly labeled make good oil containers for woods work.

When you buy a new saw, one of the first things to check is the amount of oil it uses. You can check very quickly to see if the automatic oiler is working. With the engine running fairly fast, hold the tip of the bar near a piece of paper or a fresh cut of wood. If the pump is providing oil, you will notice the oil spray onto the paper or wood. In fact, you should do this often throughout the life of the saw to make sure the oiler continues to work.

There is also another important check to be made in the beginning. See if the oil tank runs out of oil before the fuel tank runs out of fuel. If this happens, you will be running the saw toward the end of a fuel tank with the chain getting no lubrication at all. If the oiler is adjustable, take the saw to the dealer and ask him to adjust it so that the oil will last slightly longer than the fuel. Don't do it yourself because you might not give the chain enough oil. A properly equipped dealer can measure the amount of oil produced and the rpm of the engine and can adjust the amount of the oil to the specific quantity. Here again, saving a little bit of oil could be very costly in terms of chain wear. If the oil tank was simply designed too small, then you'll just have to get into the habit of never filling the fuel tank completely full. Also, if your saw has a manual oiler, be careful not to pump too much oil by hand and therefore run out of oil before the fuel runs out. If you are working under conditions that require extra oil, then stop your saw and check the oil level occasionally, rather than run the saw until the fuel runs out. Actually, it's not a bad idea to check the fuel tank often anyway. After using the saw for a while, you'll have a fairly good idea of how much fuel is left in the tank. You should never start felling a tree if there is a possibility you might run out of fuel halfway through. Stop and fill up the tank beforehand.

It's also a good idea to rinse out both the fuel and the oil tanks every month or so. You can simply empty them in an approved location. Then add a little fuel mix to both tanks, put the caps on, shake the saw, and pour that fuel out. Check the filters or strainers on both the fuel and oil pick ups; if they're okay, which they should be if you've used clean fuel and oil, you can refill the tanks and be ready to go back to work again.

Spark Plugs

Doctors routinely take their patients' temperatures as an indication of their general health. The spark plug will give the same indication of your saw's health. A plug with tan or light gray deposits tells you that everything is working fine. If the plug has a white, blistery-looking appearance, then the saw is running too hot, indicating problems with ignition timing, carburetor adjustment, or air-cooling restriction. On the other hand, a plug with heavy black deposits indicates a too rich carburetor adjustment, an improper fuel mix, or perhaps a plugged air filter. Fuel with large amounts of lead or improper lubricating oils will result in metallic deposits on the plug. Every week or so check the spark plugs and reset the gap to specifications shown in your instruction manual. Eventually, you will need a new plug when the plug electrodes erode or burn away. However, a plug in a properly operating engine lasts a long time, especially long in saws with electronic ignition. Check the spark-plug gap once a week and replace the plug if it needs it, but primarily watch that plug for signs of other engine problems.

When you do replace the spark plug, make sure you replace it with exactly the type specified by the saw's manufacturer. Plugs vary in the diameter of the threaded portion, in the length of the threaded portion, in the type of gasket or the absence of a gasket, and in the heat range. (The heat range is a measure of the plug's ability to pass heat from the electrodes out into the cylinder head where it will be cooled away.) A "hot plug" does not conduct heat as well and will run hotter in a given circumstance than will a "cold plug" which conducts heat away very rapidly. The wrong heat range for a particular engine results in a plug that either fouls very quickly because it does not burn any deposits off or runs so hot that it quickly burns out, possibly causing preignition problems in the meantime. That is, the electrodes can become so hot that they ignite the fuel-air mixture before the spark even occurs. A plug with the wrong size thread, of course, would not fit in the engine, but, on the other hand, a plug with too long a threaded length might project so far into the engine that the spark plug might hit the piston, thus causing damage. At the very least, the extra threaded length projecting into the combustion chamber could build up carbon deposits that could prevent you from ever removing the plug. Too short a plug results in improper heat flow and a lowering of the combustion ratio of the engine. In essence, make sure you get exactly the right plug the manufacturer specified.

When they install spark plugs, few loggers use torque wrenches, although they probably should. You cannot be expected to carry a torque wrench around with you, but you should at least borrow a torque wrench to determine what the proper torque feels like so that, when you put a plug in by hand, you will know how tight it should be. Overtightening the plug will distort the cylinder head, while undertightening it will result in improper sealing and improper heat flow. Again, it pays to learn the right way of installing spark plugs.

Timing

The ignition system of the saw must be properly timed so that the spark will ignite the fuel mixture in time to push the piston down. Actually, the spark does not occur at the top of the stroke. The situation is very similar to a duck hunter who does not shoot at the duck flying past but instead shoots ahead of it so that the duck and the shot pellets will arrive at the same place at the same time. In the chain saw engine, the fuel and air are ignited so that by the time the burning has progressed fairly well and the pressure has built up, the piston is at the top of the stroke and is ready to be pushed back down. If the spark occurs too early, the pressure built up by the burning fuel tries to push the piston partly back down to turn the engine over backwards. The engine may still run, but much of the heat of combustion is lost into the piston cylinder block, resulting in overheating of these parts, possibly ruining them, and in a great loss of power. If the spark occurs too late, then the fuel is still burning when the exhaust port opens, result-

Fig. 12—Some saws have timing marks on the flywheel. On most saws that do *not* have electronic ignition, by using these marks, you can set the timing in much the same way as you do an automobile.

ing in overheating of the piston and the exhaust port, possibly burning those areas, and, again, in a great loss in power. The timing in a chain saw engine with a conventional ignition system is controlled by the spacing of the breaker points. In addition, the gap between the location of the magnets on the flywheel and the magneto coils is important. Some engines have timing marks on the flywheel, while others have provision for electronic timing. Yet others have to be timed by measuring the distance the piston must go to arrive at the top of its stroke.

All in all, this is not a difficult job, with one very, very important exception. That is, the points are enclosed under the flywheel of the engine, so on most saws you must remove the flywheel in order to get to the ignition system. The flywheel of one of these engines is a delicate piece of machinery that is exposed to very rigorous conditions. Most flywheels are held onto the crankshaft by being pressed, usually by a nut on the end of the crankshaft, onto a tapered place on the crankshaft. In addition, there is usually a key to align the flywheel in the proper position. The attachment of the flywheel by the fit of the tapered crankshaft into the tapered hole in the flywheel is very accurate and sturdy. Thus, it will take a tremendous pull in order to remove the flywheel. To remove it, you must use special tools which grab onto the flywheel in specific places and jack the flywheel against the crankshaft. Generally, when the flywheel finally breaks loose, it comes off with an impressive crack, sometimes like a pistol shot. The point is, if you haven't invested in the proper tools, any attempt to get the flywheel off will almost assuredly result in damage to it. When this flywheel is rotating at 10,000 rpm, the energy stored in it is several times greater than that of a high-powered rifle. If you crack that flywheel and it breaks at that speed, you may well get it in the teeth. Hopefully, you would not toy with a loaded high-powered rifle, nor would you experiment with the flywheel unless you had the proper tools and training.

When the saw needs ignition work, take it to a dealer or buy the tools from him and have him show you how to use them. An electronic ignition system very seldom requires work, but if it does, you *have* to take it to a dealer. Trying to find the cause of the trouble with a common volt-ohm multimeter will surely destroy the electronic unit.

So the rule is this: If you think you have ignition trouble, remove the spark plug (so that you can crank the engine quickly and easily) and hold the spark plug wire ¼ inch from the cylinder block to see if there's a good healthy blue spark. If there is, and if you have no starting or spark plug troubles which might indicate poor timing, then you know the trouble lies elsewhere. If there is no spark, check the insulation on both the spark plug wire and the smaller wire that runs to the ignition switch and check the ignition switch itself to make sure that there isn't a short somewhere. If you still can't find the trouble, take the saw to a dealer. He probably can find in minutes the trouble that might take you hours to find, and he will have the proper tools to fix it.

Air Filter

Most chain saw instruction manuals suggest cleaning the air filter at least once if not twice a day under average conditions and more under extreme conditions. Many saws have their air filters cleaned only once a month. The fuel going through a saw does no good whatever unless it burns, and it cannot burn unless it has enough air. Not only will a dirty air filter result in a lack of power, but the saw also will run too rich, resulting in heavy deposits in

Fig. 13—A quick way to clean off a chain saw is with an air line. However, make sure the air line has pressure regulated according to the specifications of the Occupational Safety and Health Act (OSHA).

the engine. It also may run too hot since an ample fuel-air mixture helps to cool the saw.

It's no trouble to clean the filter. Filters can be cleaned in kerosene or gasoline, but both are dangerous, must be used outside, and are pretty messy. There's a much easier way. First of all, get an extra filter for your saw so that you don't have to clean the filter out in the field. At the end of each day, clean off the major dirt from around the carburetor and air filter (the easiest way to do this is with an air line if it's available). Put your spare filter on and bring the old one home with you. After you have eaten your supper and the dishes have been washed, take the filter apart, if it comes apart, and stick it in the soapy dishwater. Most dishwashing detergents do an excellent job of cleaning the filter and will make it look like new in no time at all. Then rinse it well and set it up where it will thoroughly dry. In the morning take it back to work and that night switch it with the other filter, which is now dirty, and repeat the process. If this is too much trouble, buy six filters and wash five of them all at once one night. This is really very little investment since filters if cleaned regularly and gently handled hardly ever wear out, and the chances are good that if you

Fig. 14—Heavy and baked-on accumulations of dirt, grease, and sawdust must be scraped off with a sharp tool, such as a screwdriver.

Fig. 15—Most air filters can be cleaned well with dishwashing detergent. They must be rinsed well and dried thoroughly before they can be placed back on the saw.

buy a new saw of the same brand these filters will fit it. So, the cost per cord of wood cut is very small. On the other hand, the benefits of having a clean filter on your saw are very great. Here again, this is another small thing that will result in more money for you in the long run.

Carburetor

The carburetor is the device that mixes the fuel with the air as it goes into the engine. It has two jobs, the mixing of the fuel in the proper ratio and the pumping of the fuel from the fuel tank to the air stream. Inside there are two little rubber sheets called diaphragms. One of these divides the compartment which is connected to the fuel line on one side and is connected to the crankcase of the engine on the other. As the piston moves up and down, the pressure inside the crankcase changes, which causes the diaphragm to vibrate back and forth. This vibrating diaphragm then sucks the fuel from the tank into the other side of the chamber and pushes it through a system of valves into another chamber of the carburetor. The second chamber acts as kind of a sack holding the fuel. As the fuel sack expands from being filled, it releases a small lever, which in turn releases a small valve, which prevents more fuel from entering. As the engine uses more fuel, the sack shrinks in size, opens the valve, and allows more fuel to enter. Thus, the engine is assured of a constant supply of fuel from a fixed location regardless of how the saw is turned—whether upside down, right side up, or any other way. However, these diaphragms do wear out from being stretched all the time, and they wear out faster if corrosives or grit gets into them from dirty fuel. In addition, dirt can plug the small passages in the carburetor and keep the small needle valve that controls the fuel flow from operating properly. It is

Fig. 16—Vacuum-pressure gauge. A chain saw carburetor can be tested with a testing kit, such as this "Flexo," or with a similar device, such as an automotive vacuum-pressure gauge. With it, you can apply both a vacuum, thus checking the carburetor diaphragm flaps, and a pressure of around 7 psi, thus checking the needle valve in the carburetor. The carburetor should hold the vacuum or pressure with only a very slow leakage. Using adapters, you can also check the crankshaft seals on the engine.

also possible that a jet of air directed toward the carburetor opening could create enough pressure inside the carburetor to burst the diaphragm.

The chain saw owner could change these diaphragms and rebuild the carburetor. Many owners in fact do, but it's a job that should be undertaken with the utmost of cleanliness, for if a small amount of dirt gets into the carburetor it could cause the carburetor to fail earlier than is normal; therefore, any money saved by the owner doing the work himself could be quickly lost through having to do the job over, and the corresponding amount of time he saved in cutting wood would also be lost.

If you do plan to do the job yourself, it is strongly suggested that you obtain a service manual for the carburetor used in your saw from the carburetor manufacturer, the saw manufacturer, or the saw dealer and that you get a man experienced in carburetor repair to work with you the first time through.

There are times when the carburetor mixture must be adjusted. If you move to a job at a considerably different elevation, you will probably need to adjust the mixture. However, many adjustments are made when they shouldn't be. So, the first step in adjustment is to make absolutely certain that the fuel filter and the air filter are clean and that the fuel tank is filled with the proper mixture of good clean fuel. Many times, after you have done this, you will decide that the carburetor really doesn't need adjusting after all.

However, if it does need adjusting, you do so by adjusting two needle valves which look like long pointed screws holding down springs. One of these valves, generally the one closest to the engine itself, controls the fuel mixture when the engine is idling. The second valve, generally the one closest to the air filter, controls the fuel mixture when the engine is running at high speed under load. In addition, there is a third adjustment, a set screw (with a spring to keep it from unscrewing) which bears against the throttle control to adjust the idle speed.

Once again, it's best to have the dealer do the adjustment, but since the dealer isn't always available, here's how to go about it. First, if you have completely disassembled the carburetor, very gently screw both needle valves in until they stop. Don't force them or you'll ruin the whole carburetor. Unscrew each needle one turn. Now start the saw up and keep it running or restart it several times until the engine is warmed up. Tune the idle-speed

Fig. 17—Side view of a Tillotson carburetor, the most popular type of chain saw today. The screw heads for the fuel-mixture adjustment needle are at the bottom, the left one being the low-speed jet, the right one being the high-speed jet. Note the "L" and the "H" molded into the carburetor body. The idle-speed adjustment screw is at the top right of the carburetor. This particular model has a collar around the head of the screw so that the screwdriver will not slip out of the slot when you are adjusting it with the engine running. The throttle-trigger linkage is attached to the odd-shaped plate, with the holes on the upper left side of the carburetor. When the carburetor is mounted on a chain saw, the air filter is attached to the right side of this carburetor and the engine block is to the right.

jet with the engine idling until the engine sounds the best and is running the fastest. You may have to change the idle speed setting again. What you want is as fast an idle speed as you can get without there being any chance of the clutch engaging and the chain moving.* Now hold the throttle open and adjust the main-speed

———————

*If the chain tends to move at a very low idle speed or even all the time, then you may have a clutch problem. Sometimes as a saw gets old, the clutch spring loses its strength and allows the weights to move out too easily, or a piece breaks off the clutch and jams it, or the clutch just gets packed up with sawdust and dirt and gets jammed that way. Clean the clutch out, look for broken parts, and if you can't find anything wrong, take it to a dealer.

jet. As you back the jet out more and more, the saw will get too rich and falter, and eventually if you go too far, it will stall. As you screw the jet slowly back in, the engine will run faster and faster and suddenly will sound as if it takes a slight jump in speed—that is, it will start "screaming." As far as the main-speed jet is concerned, you do *not* want the setting that gives you the highest rpm because you will not get the greatest power that way—when you're limbing, the rpm may get so high that it will destroy the saw. When the engine is running just slightly too rich, it will start to "four cycle." That is, it will have a rough, ragged sound, as if it's firing every other stroke. Screwing the jet in just a little bit will clear it so that it will run fast and smooth. You want to set it right there. When you think you've got it, try cutting with the saw. The saw should have plenty of power. If it doesn't, try richening out just a little bit, but don't let the engine run rough. But, under a load, with the throttle held open, it shouldn't scream either.

Really the best way to adjust engine speed would be to tune the main speed jet with the engine under load. Trying to do this while cutting wood is extremely dangerous. Some progressive dealers have *dynamometers*, big fans driven by a belt. The dealer can clamp the saw down and adjust the engine under load that way.

Once you think you have the main-speed jet set right, then go back to the idle adjustment to recheck it, and adjust the idle speed if necessary. When you think you've got the whole thing adjusted properly, try two more checks. First, with the engine idling, quickly open the throttle. If the engine falters or stalls, richen it out slightly by screwing the idle-speed screw out a slight amount and try it again. When you've got that, hold the saw when it's idling and turn it over on its side as you would when you fell a tree. Then turn it back again to the bucking position, then back to the felling position. If the engine stalls under these conditions, lean out the idling mixture by screwing the idle screw in slightly. When you can turn the saw around without it stalling, when it accelerates quickly from idle, has plenty of power when cutting, doesn't scream too fast with no load, and doesn't idle fast enough to cause the chain to move, then it will undoubtedly start right off on the first pull as well, and you can consider your tuning job a success. Nevertheless, you can double check yourself again by checking the appearance of the spark plug after you have run the saw an hour or so.

Starter

Most saws are started by a rope with a "T"-handle wound onto a drum with a spring to recoil the rope after starting. The starter pulley is connected to the flywheel either by pawls on the flywheel which automatically disengage themselves by centrifugal action once the engine starts or by pawls on the starter pulley which are cammed out against the inside of a drum on the flywheel by the action of pulling the starter rope. The best maintenance for a starter cord is simply proper use. The starter rope should never be snapped out. Always pull the cord slowly

Fig. 18—The starter rope should always be pulled straight out and guided straight back in by hand in order to keep the housing from being worn.

until the starter pawls catch and then quickly pull the cord straight out so that it does not wear against the side of the starter casing. After pulling the rope, don't let it snap back in; instead, guide it in with your hand. If you pull the rope at an angle, it will wear the rope out very rapidly, and the rope will eventually wear a hole

Fig. 19—Replacing a starter rope is easy. Run the new rope into the pulley and tie a knot on the end.

Fig. 20—There is generally a notch in the pulley so that the free end can be brought into the notch while the pulley is turned around and around to get proper tension.

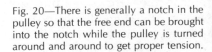

Fig. 21—To check tension, pull the rope all the way out and hold it with one hand while, at the same time, continuing to turn the starter pulley another half turn if you can.

right down through the starter casing, almost as though it were a file. A quick snap that makes the starter pawls catch suddenly can mean rapid wear on the pawls and the starter pulley, and surprisingly, letting the rope snap back in on its own can be the most expensive blunder of all. Sometimes the rope gets a quick jerk from the spring, which sends it back into the housing faster than the recoil can wind it onto the pulley. It's possible on some saws for the rope to get off the pulley and into the flywheel housing. If a loop of the rope should then get caught around one of the starter pawls, it can yank the pawl and its attaching stud right out of the flywheel. This will necessitate a new flywheel, which is an expensive repair. This same problem can occur if the starter spring becomes dirty and gummy, thus loosening the rope inside the flywheel housing. Consequently, a couple times a year completely clean out the starter spring. Then lubricate it with either dry graphite or special silicone lubricant.

Replacing the starter rope is an easy repair. However, make sure that the spring is properly tensioned. When you pull the rope all the way out, it should still be possible to turn the starter pulley an additional half to three-quarters turn. If you cannot turn it this much, you may stretch the spring too tightly and break it. If you haven't tensioned it enough, you may get into the troubles already mentioned. Make sure that you replace the screws holding the starter housing to the engine securely. It's a good idea to use "Loctite," a chemical made to keep screws from loosening (it can be bought at a hardware or auto parts store). However, you can usually take the screws out with tools, and if not, you can apply heat to loosen them.

Bar and Chain Maintenance

The chain saw manufacturers provide excellent free booklets on chain and bar maintenance. By all means get one. Not only do these booklets give many tips in order for you to get more life and faster cutting from your chain, but they also give step-by-step instructions when you have heavy filing to do—for example, if you should hit a rock.

However, the most important part of filing a chain is very simple and contributes greatly to chain life. That is, every time you fill up your saw with fuel, touch up the chain. This is done with nothing more than a round file of the proper size. After a

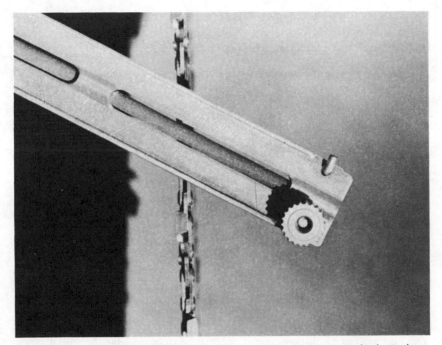

Fig. 22—Use a file holder to do heavy filing. This is the new Oregon style shown here. Note that there are angle guide marks for both the chisel-and older chipper-style chains.

little practice you won't need a file holder since all you do is fit the file into the tooth at the angle that's already there and take one nice firm stroke to maintain the cutting edge. The amount of metal that you have to remove is extremely minute, but it will maintain the sharpness of the chain. If you ignore this filing, the saw will get dull and you will really have to take metal off in order to get it back into shape or you may lose the angle. Consequently, it's a good idea to use a file guide.

Some men run a finger over the top edge of their saw teeth, find them sharp, and don't bother to touch them up. They may be getting fooled. The top part of the tooth may be sharp, but it won't make much difference if it isn't—it doesn't do much anyway. Most of the cutting and 80 percent of the horsepower expended in the chain go into the corner where the side plate and the top plate come together. If this corner is dull, then it will have a large effect on the speed of cutting of the chain. Besides, it will quickly hammer itself back to where you have to take off a large amount of metal in order to get it sharp again. Since this corner dulls first, a quick glance at the top plate to see if it's sharp doesn't really matter. Always make sure that the *corner* is sharp.

Fig. 23—Touching up the teeth on a saw in the woods is easy with just a file with a handle. Just make sure to fit the file to the tooth configuration. On the new style chisel chains, do not hold the file horizontally—hold it about 10 degrees below horizontal.

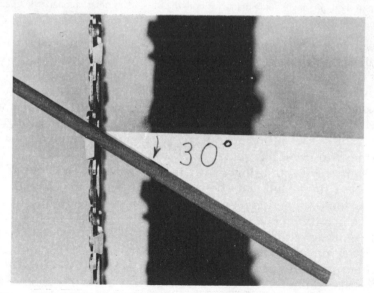

Fig. 24—Chisel chains are filed with a 30-degree top-plate angle.

After you have touched up the teeth four or five times, check the depth gauges with a depth-gauge tool to make sure that they are all set at the proper setting. Do *not* set your depth gauges any lower than factory specifications. Though it seems as if you're cutting faster because the saw is jumping and growling away, you actually aren't, as you can prove to yourself by trying to cut with a

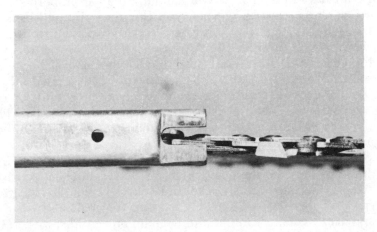

Fig. 25—A depth-gauge joining tool shown on a chain. Note that on the new anti-kick chains the slot in the joining tool must be wide enough to accommodate both the depth gauge and the safety ramp. An older tool with a narrower slot will ride up on the safety ramp and will give a false reading.

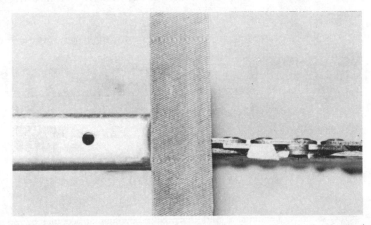

Fig. 26—File off any part of the depth gauge which projects above the joining tool. Then remove the joiner and file the front corner of the depth gauge so that it is rounded. A sharp corner would catch and chatter when you are cutting wood.

new chain and then timing yourself again after lowering the depth gauge. This extra vibration will do your hands no good. Furthermore, lowered depth gauges are a major cause of chain kickback accidents.

After the bar has been used for some time, the moving chain works a burr onto the edge of the guide rail. This burr sticks out from both sides of the bar. If you maintain the bar properly, when a cut first starts to pinch the bar, you can generally pull back on the bar with the engine running, and the saw will cut itself back out. However, if there is a burr on the bar, the closing kerf will catch on that burr, and it will be difficult if not impossible to get the bar back out. So, weekly, file that burr off. It's a good idea to turn the bar over every day or so, so that you cut for a while on one side and then you cut for a while on the other side of the bar. That way, you even out the wear, and you don't wear a bumpy hollow on one side of the bar.

Sprockets are a greatly neglected part of the saw. Of course, the sprocket must be the right pitch for the chain. That is, given the size of the chain, the sprocket must be the right size for it. As the sprocket wears, it gets smaller. Because the chain also wears as the sprocket wears, if you put a new chain on an old sprocket, the pitch doesn't match. You'll find it hard to keep the chain tensioned (since it doesn't fit right if the chain is at the proper tension), and it won't be able to turn. If the chain will turn, it's too loose. In addition, the chain can become work hardened by the hammering

Fig. 27—Cross sections of chain saw guide bars. Note how the bar becomes burred after having been used awhile. This burr must be filed off so that the width of the bar will be less than the width of the kerf cut by the chain.

Fig. 28—Using a flat file, file the burr off the edge of the guide bar at least once a week.

Fig. 29—If you do not have the proper tools to hold the crankshaft from turning, you may have a hard time getting the clutch or flywheel nuts off. Don't try to jam the flywheel with something, for you'll damage it. On most saws you can remove the spark plug and fill the top part of the piston with a piece of clean starter rope. When the piston comes up, it cannot compress the rope, and it will keep the crankshaft from turning without damaging anything. Leave some of the rope sticking out so that you can remove it easily afterwards.

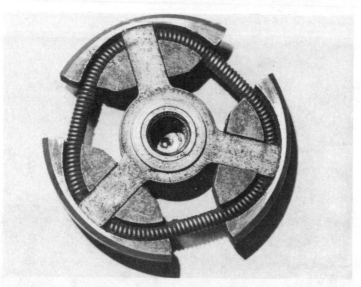

Fig. 30—A coiled spring holds the clutch shoes in away from the clutch drum when the engine is idling. If you can't get your engine to idle at the proper speed without the chain turning, check to make sure this spring is not stretched or broken. Also look for broken pieces of clutch shoes and dirt and other foreign matter that might wedge these parts together.

Fig. 31—A tiny amount of grease applied to the needle bearings in the clutch drum once a week will lubricate these parts.

the sprocket gives it. If you take a piece of wire and bend it back and forth, it becomes harder and harder to bend. As it becomes harder and harder, it also gets more brittle and eventually breaks off. Under the pounding given it by a mismatched sprocket, the chain links become work hardened and more brittle, and eventually they crack and then the chain breaks. At the least you have to replace the chain. If you are unlucky, that chain may whip around and hurt you when it breaks. As a general rule, always put on a new sprocket when you put on a new chain. One way to stretch sprocket life is to use two chains and one sprocket. Alternate the chains every other day so that the chains and sprocket wear together. Again, the sprocket presents an opportunity for false economy. You can save the price of a sprocket by never replacing the sprocket, but you may replace many more chains.

When you get a new chain, soak it in oil the night before. Then put it on the saw and run it at half throttle without cutting for four or five minutes. Let it cool, recheck the tension, and make a few light cuts. Check the tension often during the first day. This way the chain rivets wear in slowly. Each rivet is a small bearing and has to wear in somewhat before mating properly. As the rivets wear in, the chain will appear to stretch, and the tension will be lost. If you don't break in the chain properly, it will wear out prematurely, and that will mean more cost per amount of wood cut.

Fig. 32—When adjusting chain tension, lift the *tip* of the bar. The chain should be as tight as you can get it, but yet it should be loose enough so that you can, by using two fingers, pull the chain around the bar smoothly.

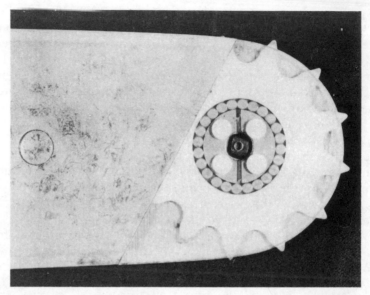

Fig. 33—A cut-away view of a sprocket-nosed chain saw bar. Note the tiny rollers which must receive adequate lubrication if they are to perform their job well.

Here is the proper way to adjust chain tension. Loosen the bar nuts slightly so that you can move the bar by hand. Since the bar fits somewhat loosely on the bar studs, hold the *tip* of the bar up with one hand while you adjust the chain-adjusting screw with the other. The proper tension on either a sprocket-nosed or hard-tipped bar is such that you can just pull the chain around the bar smoothly by hand. Any tighter and you'll loose too much power to friction, and you may damage the crankshaft of the saw. Any looser and the chain will hammer the bar and dish out places, ruining the bar, as well as making it more prone to cause the saw to kick back.

Finally, check yourself. Under average conditions, you should be getting at least 200 cords or 100,000 board-feet of wood cut per chain. Unfortunately, many loggers through their own fault get much, much less.

General Maintenance

The following schedule of maintenance will eliminate most major chain saw repairs and resulting down time.

When the saw is new:

1. Read the instruction manual.
2. Copy down the model and serial number of your saw, the length of the bar, and the number of drive links on the chain. Place this piece of paper in your wallet so you'll always have it when you go to get a new part.
3. Check the saw over to make sure that it's properly assembled and all screws and bolts are tight.
4. Break in the chain properly, as will be discussed later.

Every time the saw is refueled:

1. Add clean bar and chain oil to the saw first so you don't forget.
2. Swirl the fuel in the can to make sure it is well mixed before adding it to the saw.
3. Touch up the cutters on the chain with a round file.
4. When the bar has cooled some, check to make sure the tension is all right.
5. If you have a sprocket-nosed or roller-tipped bar, grease it.
6. After starting the saw, check to see that oil is being added to the chain by holding the bar near some light-colored object to see if oil is thrown off.

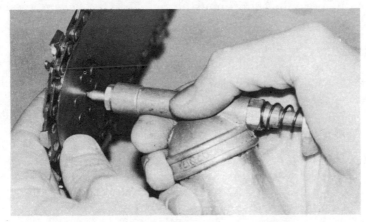

Fig. 34—Be sure to grease sprocket-nosed and roller-tipped bars with a needle-tip grease gun every time you fill the saw with gas and again at the end of the day. Make sure the gun is actually pumping grease. Some guns feel as if they are pumping when they actually are not. The gun shown here is a good reliable type that can be cleaned easily.

Once a day:

1. Clean the air filter.
2. Clean the chain guide groove and oil hole in the bar.
3. Clean the cylinder cooling pins and all the rest of the saw. (In a saw producing about 4 horsepower to the cutting chain, about 8 horsepower is lost as heat energy. If the saw is not kept clean, that heat remains in the engine and builds up the temperature, thus causing more rapid wear.)
4. If you have a sprocket-nosed or roller-tipped bar, grease it at the end of the day.
5. Turn the cutting bar over.
6. Check all screws and nuts in the saw to make sure they are tight.
7. Store your saw in a safe place where there will not be a great change in temperature. If you have been working out where it's cold, don't bring the saw into a warm building or into the warm cab of a truck—moisture will condense on it.

Weekly:

1. Lubricate the clutch bearing. (There are very few saws that don't require this.)
2. Clean the guide bar and file the burr from its edge.
3. Check and if necessary clean and adjust the spark plug.
4. Remove the starter housing and clean the fan and the housing.

Monthly maintenance:

1. Rinse out the oil and fuel tanks.
2. Clean the strainers or filters on the oil and fuel pick-up hoses inside the tanks.
3. Check the recoil starter. Change the starting rope if it appears frayed. Don't wait until it breaks out on the job.

Four or five times a year:

1. Check the ignition timing.
2. Take an older saw to the dealer and have him check the compression, oil pump function, etc.

Never:

1. Run the saw with broken parts or missing screws or bolts. This will surely add up to greater repairs later.

TROUBLE SHOOTING

Problem	Possible Cause	Remedy
Engine will not start.	Empty fuel tank.	Fill with proper mixture.
	Flooded.	Release choke. Remove and dry spark plug and crank several times. Replace plug and try to start with wide open throttle.
	Water or dirt in fuel.	Replace with clean fuel. Fuel filter may have to be replaced.
	Carburetor improperly adjusted (likely only if tampered with).	See instruction manual or dealer.
	Spark plug fouled.	Clean or replace. Check fuel mixture and make sure air filter is clean. Check that plug is of proper heat range.
	Plug wires grounded.	Reroute wires and insulate with tape or replace.
	Faulty switch.	Replace. (Check by disconnecting wire from switch and starting saw—choke to stop.)
	Faulty timing.	See dealer.
	Burned points.	See dealer.
	Defective electronic ignition unit.	See dealer. (Don't try to test.)
Engine is hard to start.	Improper fuel mix.	Replace with proper mix.
	Fouled plug.	Replace or clean.
	Dirty fuel or air filters.	Clean or replace.
	Improper carburetor adjustment.	See dealer or instruction manual.
	Faulty timing.	See dealer.
Engine floods.	Carburetor needle stuck or faulty.	See dealer.
	Carburetor diaphragm torn.	See dealer.
Engine quits or misfires.	Short in ignition system.	Find short and insulate with tape or replace wire.
	Fouled plug.	Clean or replace. (Check fuel mixture.)
	Faulty timing.	See dealer.

(Continued)

TROUBLE SHOOTING (Continued)

Problem	Possible Cause	Remedy
Engine quits or misfires.	Faulty points.	See dealer.
	Dirt packed outside carburetor diaphragm.	Clean. (May need dealer's help if sawdust is inside carburetor cover plate.)
	Fuel tank vent clogged or sticking.	Clean or replace.
Chain moves at idle.	Idle speed set too high.	Adjust.
	Clutch spring stretched.	Replace.
	Clutch shoe broken.	Replace.
	Clutch jammed.	Clean.
Engine lacks power. (Check: Does it really lack power or is chain improperly maintained?)	Incorrect fuel mix.	Replace with correct fuel mix.
	Incorrect carburetor adjustment.	See dealer or instruction manual.
	Dirty air or fuel filters.	Clean.
	Cooling air plugged.	Clean cylinder fins and rest of saw.
	Cylinder ports clogged with carbon.	Remove muffler and carefully clean with wooden paddle. Check fuel mixture and carburetor setting, and make sure proper engine oil is being used. Keep air filter clean.
	Worn cylinder and rings.	See dealer.
Engine starves on acceleration.	Improper carburetor setting.	See dealer or instruction manual.
	Muffler loose.	Check gasket and tighten.
	Air leak into crankcase (especially worn crankshaft seals).	See dealer.

CHAPTER 3

Saw Technique

Like the student who practices driving a car in an empty parking lot before he drives in traffic, you should learn how to make your saw do whatever you want it to do before you actually start felling, limbing, and bucking trees. For example, when you are felling a tree, there are many factors you must consider for your own safety and for good production. If you have to think about how to make the saw cut the way you want it to without hurting yourself, then you may overlook something else important and end up being injured. There are proper techniques to use in order to get a saw to cut the way you want it to, regardless of the situation.

Clothing

The saw isn't the only piece of equipment you need to be a logger. There are many other accessories, most of which could be loosely termed "clothing," that you will need to do your job effectively and safely. One of the items you will need is a hard hat. Make sure it's a safety hat—a hat that has a tag "ANSI Z89.1"—not just a "bump cap." A safety hat or helmet is designed to protect your head from falling objects. A "helmet"-type hat called a "bump cap" looks similar to a safety hat but is primarily intended to protect a man's head when he's working in an area with a low ceiling. It's not adequate for the job of logging. In winter months in the North woods, you also may want to get helmet liners that go inside the hard hat and keep your ears and head warm.

Generally, for body clothing it's better to have several layers of light clothing than one big heavy coat, because as you work, you'll warm up and you'll want to be able to adjust your temperature. All clothing should be loose enough to allow freedom of movement but yet not be floppy—you don't want it catching in brush and limbs. Many loggers "stag" or cut off the bottom few inches of their pants to keep the pants from catching.

You should consider wearing ballistic nylon knee protectors. These are pads made of several layers of strong nylon cloth which are worn over the knee area. They are designed to give you more "reaction time" if the saw were to accidentally cut through the protector and to jam the saw chain and prevent it from cutting you as badly as it might if the moving chain were to touch your leg without the pad.

There are many ways of attaching the pads. Some pads have straps around the leg, some have buttons or snaps to be snapped to the inside of the pants, and some specially made pants have pockets for pads. One of the best methods found so far is to buy pads with Velcro strips on them and to attach them to Velcro strips sewn inside your pants. ("Velcro" is a patented material that sticks

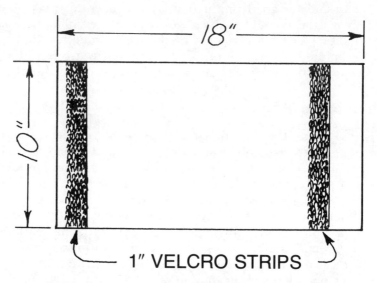

Fig. 35—Safety knee pads made of ballistic nylon or some other special material should be no smaller than this in order to provide adequate protection. Many men prefer pads made longer but tapered to a smaller width at the bottom to fit more easily in pants. The Velcro tapes shown here are a good way to attach the pads inside the logger's pants.

Fig. 36—Velcro strips sewn inside the logger's pants and on the safety knee patches provide an easy way of attaching the pads. The pads can be easily switched to another pair of pants when that pair is being washed.

to a special tape. It can be bought at sewing centers.) When attached this way, the pads do not sag, are easily removed when the pants are washed, and can be used in several pairs of pants; in addition, there are no uncomfortable buttons or snaps when you're kneeling. Large "chap"-type pads undoubtedly give more protection, but they're hot in the summer, are clumsy, and restrict movement. Your pants should also have large stout pockets in back that will not be torn off by the weight of carrying wedges in them. You should have good stout boots that give firm ankle support and that have non-slip soles and safety toe caps. Modern safety boots have padding inside so that the caps won't bother your toes. Insulated or fiber caps are available for winter use so that your toes won't get cold. The steel caps don't seem to add materially to boot wear, provided you keep the boots well oiled. Boots are also available with tongues and insteps covered with ballistic nylon protection against chain cuts.

Depending upon the make of the saw and the work you are doing (whether you're bucking in the woods, bucking on a yard, felling, etc.), you may or may not need ear protection. In general, there are three types available. The first is "Swedish Wool," a very fine fiberglass material that feels like slippery cotton and that is rolled into plugs and placed in the ears. At the end of the day, these are thrown out. Cotton is by no means a substitute for this substance. Also, make certain that you roll the plugs as illustrated on the box so that you don't have ragged pieces of the wool left inside your ears. This substance is effective, but some men complain of the "noise" that is made—sort of a creaking when you move your head. The second type of ear protection is a specially designed ear plug made out of plastic that is placed in the ear, can be taken out at night, and can be washed and reused. It is light and comfortable in summer use. The third type is a special kind of ear muff which looks like radio headphones, except there are no wires attached. It is the most effective of all, but is sometimes considered too warm in the summer. Furthermore, you must make sure that any ear protection you use fits right—a poor seal will prevent your being protected.

You should also have some form of eye protection. Chips and splinters are thrown by the saw. Even if you don't receive a painful injury from one of these, the dust in the air can cause abrasion of the eyeball. You can use face masks made of various substances, or you may use eyeglasses. The face-mask type of protector has clear plastic (which may become scratched and dirty) or nylon or wire screen mesh. The wire screen may be smoked over a candle to prevent reflection, so that it is almost invisible when you are using it. However, face masks may prove troublesome in the North woods during the black fly season. Safety glasses made of both glass and plastic are available. If prescription lenses are necessary (determined by your eye doctor), the plastic type may give greater protection from blows if your eyes require the lens to be ground to a prescription that results in very thin areas. The plastic type is also lighter and less likely to fog. On the other hand, tempered optical glass may not scratch as easily.

You will also need gloves or mitts to protect your hands. Leather gloves are available with ballistic nylon on the back of the left hand to protect it against chain saw kickbacks. Even with a chain brake, some type of padding is suggested to cushion the hand used to trip the chain brake, since it will be used often to lock the chain when traveling, to start the saw, etc.

You probably will also need wedges made of aluminum, magnesium, or plastic that will not damage the chain if it should strike them. Plastic wedges are now available with cross ridges which

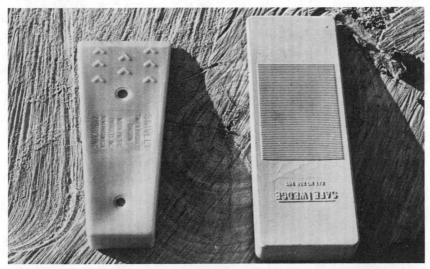

Fig. 37—New types of plastic wedges will not harm the chain if it is struck, and they have ridges or teeth to help keep the wedge from slipping back out of the tree when it is being used with frozen wood.

tend to prevent the wedge from kicking back out of the kerf when being driven into frozen wood. Of course, a single-bit ax or light sledge hammer is necessary to drive the wedges. Alternately, you may decide to use a Scandinavian log breaker on smaller timber in place of the ax and wedges. The use of these tools will be covered in Chapter 4.

Starting the Saw

Before you can use the saw, of course, you have to start it. The best way is to place the saw on the ground, with your left hand on the front handlebar holding the saw firmly and your right foot through the rear handlebar so that the saw cannot move. Now grab the starter rope and slowly pull it straight up out of the hole. (If you don't pull it straight, you will cause rapid wear on the saw and on the rope.) Keep pulling it slowly until you feel the pawls (the parts that connect the starter to the engine) engage. When the starter is engaged, give the rope a quick, sharp pull, and the engine should start. If you yank the rope quickly all the way from the start, the starter pawls will engage with a crash and will cause rapid wear and strain on these parts.

Individual saws differ somewhat in exactly how they must be treated for quick starting, but generally a saw should have the chain brake set on, throttle lock halfway open, and, when the engine is cold, the choke on. After you have pulled the rope a couple of times, the engine will start and then flood out and die down. Push the choke in; then pull the cord again, and the saw should run. As soon as the saw starts, squeeze and release the trigger so that the throttle is no longer held halfway open. Otherwise, with the chain brake engaged, you'll cause rapid wear on the clutch. After the engine has been running for awhile and is warm, the saw should start without a choke and without the throttle being locked halfway open.

Although starting the saw on the ground is definitely the best way, it's not always practical. You certainly can't do this when there is a great depth of powder snow. Besides, it takes time to put the saw down every time you want to start it. Another good method is to hold the saw with the rear handlebar between your legs. Your left hand holds the front handlebar at the top left corner so that the saw is tilted toward the right. Now, when you pull the starter rope with your right hand, the rope will come straight out, and the pull of the saw will act against your left hand and your right leg. Note again that the pull is not straight *up* but rather straight *out* from the saw (which is tilted halfway toward the right).

There are two other methods for starting the saw which are widely used. One is to hold the saw by the rear handlebar in the right hand and pull the starter rope with the left hand. In the days before most saws had throttle latches, this was often necessary. With a heavy saw with a long bar, say 36 inches or longer, it works quite well, as you can rest the bar over a log or stump—the mass of the heavy saw will provide enough inertia so that you can yank the starter rope out all right. On a lightweight saw, this doesn't work. The only way to make it work is to more or less "throw" the saw with the right hand, pulling back at the same time at the left. Of course, if your hand should slip off the starter rope and the saw should start, then the saw is aimed down towards your right leg (remember your right hand is holding the throttle open, or else it is locked open by the half-throttle latch). Obviously, this method could cause a severe leg injury.

The other method that is often used is to hold the saw with the left hand at the top of the front handlebar and pull the starter

Fig. 38—Here is a good safe way to start a chain saw when you can't place it directly on the ground (as when there is deep snow). Hold the saw at about a 45-degree angle and pull the starter rope straight out from the housing. This way the housing and the rope do not get worn. The pull is not straight up, but since the saw is tilted, the force is directed against the right leg.

rope with the right hand, or so it seems at first glance. Actually, if you just hold your left hand still, you will find that the inertia of the saw is not great enough and all you'll succeed in doing is pulling the saw so that the bar hits your left leg while you're pulling on the starter rope. In actual practice, you will notice that the men who use this method "throw" the saw toward the ground with their left hand (while still holding firmly onto it) and, at the same time, snap the starter rope sharply upward with their right. The saw stays horizontal, and few men seem to get hurt. Note however that the starter rope is jerked out rapidly. The men who use this method may wonder why they have to change their starter ropes so often, why starter pawls and flywheel dogs wear out so often, and why they break so many starter springs.

Holding the Saw

Assuming that you have used the first method to start the saw, your left hand is already on the front handlebar. All you have to do now is grip the rear handlebar with your right hand and you're ready to cut. But, there are a few techniques to consider here too.

First of all, make sure that your feet are comfortably apart, with one ahead of the other so that you have a firm base to support yourself. Second, whenever possible, lean against the tree that you are working on in order to give yourself even better support. When cutting, always hold the saw with both hands—but don't overdo it. If you hold the saw with extreme firmness, you will feel the vibrations transmitted from the saw to a greater extent; thus, you will become fatigued, and you may lose control. Think of automobile drivers: The new driver holds the steering wheel in a "death grip." The poor driver drapes one hand over the wheel. The good driver holds the wheel so that he is in control but is relaxed and uses no more force than necessary. It's the same thing with a chain saw. The saw is actually steered by the handlebars, and your grip should be about the same as on the steering wheel of a car. If you have to hold the saw tightly and force it to work, something is wrong. Most likely your chain is not filed correctly. Don't ever force the saw; instead, guide it to do what you want. Your left thumb should be *underneath* the front handlebar and not on the top, so that if the saw should kick, the saw is more likely to be jammed back into the web of the thumb and fingers, and you will have a chance to try to control it. If the thumb is on the top of the handlebar and the saw kicks, the saw will go right on by and your hand is apt to end up in the chain.

Kickback: It appears that the greatest number of injuries in the woods today are due to chain saw accidents. And, apparently, the greatest number of chain saw injuries are cuts, and the greatest number of cuts are due to kickback. Although there are a number of dangers in the woods which must be guarded against, if you had to choose just one thing to avoid it well might be the kickback.

What has a linked chain guided in a more or less oval path, powered by an internal combustion engine through a drive sprocket? Why, a crawler tractor, of course. Would you have said chain saw? Well, of course, you would have been right there too, for both these machines are essentially similar. With the tractor, the idea is not to let the chain slip in contact with the object it is resting on, so that the reaction causes the whole machine to move forward. With a chain saw, the idea is just the opposite. The chain saw is not supposed to move forward because of the reaction, but rather the chain is supposed to slip over (and cut) the object it is resting on. Unfortunately, if the chain takes too big a bite, it has a tendency to want to become a tractor. Thus, kickback really occurs any place on the guide bar. When you're cutting with the bottom of the guide bar, the saw will tend to be drawn forward towards the bumper spikes. When you're cutting with the top of the bar, the saw will tend to be pushed back towards you. The real trouble occurs when the chain on the upper quarter of the nose of the bar (between "12 and 3 o'clock") hits some object. When this happens, the nose of the bar is pushed upward slightly. However, be-

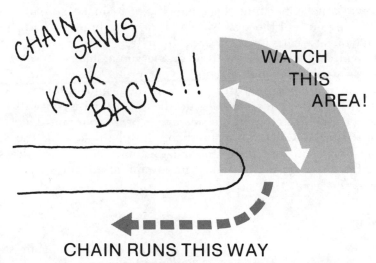

CHAIN RUNS THIS WAY

Fig. 39 This part of the nose of the bar is more likely to cause kickback than any other. Be very careful that this part of the saw doesn't contact something accidentally.

cause of the curvature of the bar, just as soon as the bar moves upward even the slightest degree, it actually pushes harder at the object; therefore, the bar has even more of a tendency to come up, and as it comes up more, it pushes harder towards the object, which, in turn, causes it to kick even harder. In considerably less than a tenth of a second, the saw is flying back upward towards you. Remember, your reaction time is probably slower than a tenth of a second, and when you're tired, it is sure to be. So, your chances of stopping that saw are really small. Quite often, in fact, you may even help it kick inadvertently. Suppose, for example, you are using the top of the bar to limb along a tree. You are pulling on the handlebar, pulling the chain up against the limb; whereas actually, you are also pulling the saw towards yourself. If it should hit a branch on the ground or a rock or some other object, the saw will kick towards you—you will not have time to stop it, for you actually will be pulling the saw and helping it to come towards you faster.

There are three things you can do to help prevent kickback. First of all, get a chain brake on your saw. Chain brakes are designed to work faster than your reaction time, so even though the saw may still hit you, at least the chain won't be moving. Of course, you have to check that chain brake often to make sure that it is working. (Checking the chain brake to make sure it works each time you fuel the saw is a good idea.) Using the chain brake when you are carrying your saw from tree to tree protects you while you are moving, as well as giving you a chance to see if the brake is working or not. Second, wear protective clothing. Wear gloves or mitts with ballistic nylon in them and protective knee pads. If the saw "tries" to cut into these materials, you will have some reaction time to pull the saw away, or, in some instances, the nylon material will grab enough of the chain to stop the saw. Either way, you will have enough reaction time to get the saw away from you. Third, and most important, at all times *watch the nose of the bar*.

Cutting

When learning to write, you may have had a teacher stand over you with a ruler who made you fill many pages with nice round "o's" and nice straight "i's." Before you could learn to draw letters, you had to learn to control the pen. Similarly, before you decide to fell a tree, you ought to learn how to make the saw do what you want it to do. There are only three cuts which can be made with the chain saw. Whether you are felling, bucking, limbing, or carving a statue, only these three cuts are used (but in various combinations).

Pulling chain cut: It is accomplished with the lower edge of the guide bar. The reaction force is such that the saw is pulled forward. So, whenever possible, let it. Put the bumper plate or "bucking" (or "bark" or "bumper") spikes on the saw right up against the tree and use them to lever the saw into the wood. But, don't force the saw—let the chain cut its own way through the tree. If you have to push it through, then it needs to be sharpened. Generally, let the bucking spikes hold the engine of the saw in one place while the tip of the bar cuts down into the log somewhat. Then, while keeping the nose of the bar in the same place, pull the bucking spikes back slightly and let the engine end of the guide bar cut in to some degree. Let the saw pull itself back in and let the nose cut some more. In this way the guide bar is kind of "walked" through a large cut.

When you are cutting a small log or limb, the saw can usually cut right through in one smooth strike. Therefore, saws that are used primarily for cutting small wood quite often don't have bucking spikes. This can be unfortunate because they can be useful when felling.

The pulling chain cut is the easiest cut of all to make. In fact, you really could control the saw with just one hand on the rear handlebar—but that's not recommended because when bucking a log you may at times lose sight of the nose of the bar. If that nose comes in contact with something, then you'll have a kickback, and with no hand on the front handlebar, you will have no way to stop the saw. In fact, you don't even have any way to trip the chain brake on—so always keep both hands on the saw.

Pushing chain cut: It is made by using the chain on the top of the guide bar. A sprocket nose is a great help in the pushing chain cut because it cuts down on the friction as the chain travels over the nose of the bar; therefore, the chain runs cooler and holds its tension better. You have to work a little harder at this kind of cut because the reaction to the cutting will push the saw back out of the cut towards you. In a pulling chain cut, you can let the chain pull the saw right up to the engine and then the engine will hold

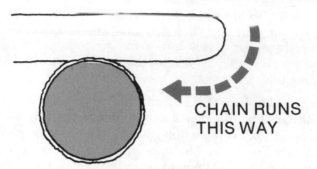

Fig. 40—Cutting with a pulling chain.

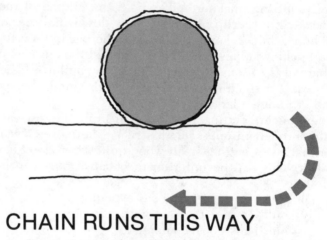

Fig. 41—Cutting with a pushing chain or "underbucking."

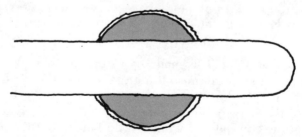

Fig. 42—A finished plunge cut results in the bar of the saw going right into the tree, leaving wood on both sides.

the saw there. In the pushing chain cut, you have to hold the saw. Besides, if you're cutting from the bottom of a log, you'll have to hold the weight of the saw too. Other than that, this cut is not that much different from the pulling chain cut. The only real danger to this cut lies in letting the saw come out too far from the cut because the nose of the bar is then in a position to cause kickback.

Boring or plunge cut: It is made by cutting with the nose of the bar. Needless to say, this is dangerous. You know by now the saw will definitely kick. Consequently, in this cut you must use proper technique or you are going to get hurt. If you were to try to place the bar perpendicular to the log and cut right in, it would immediately kick back. The trick is to cut a "pocket" in the wood before you start cutting straight in. Once you have a small pocket cut in the tree, and although the bar tries to kick, it's all surrounded by wood, and you won't get hurt.

There are two ways to cut this starting pocket. One is to use the bottom side of the end of the bar and cut with it until you get a pocket made that will contain the nose of the bar. Of course, the saw tries to kick some but what it does is kick away from contact with the tree, and as soon as it does, it doesn't have any real power. So, you just hold it up against the tree and cut away until you've cut the pocket. The second way is to use the top side of the nose of the bar, making sure that you get past the 12 o'clock posi-

Fig. 43—Don't start the saw this way—it will kick!

tion. The guide bar should be as nearly parallel to the tree as you can make it, at least when you start. This way the saw's tendency is to kick the nose of the bar into the tree—which is what you want anyway. Again, once you have the pocket cut, you can slowly swing the engine end of the saw around until you are cutting

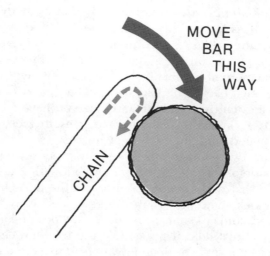

Fig. 44—This is one way to start the pocket. Once you have a pocket cut in the tree to hold the nose of the bar, then you can cut on in straight.

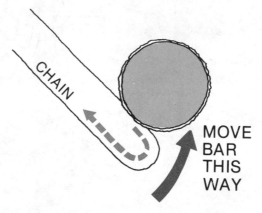

Fig. 45—You can also start the pocket this way, but stay away from the nose of the bar at first, for the saw may kick out.

straight in, and then you can send the bar right on through the tree if you wish. Once the nose of the bar is inside the pocket, it can't kick.

Practice

Yes, practice makes perfect. Practice these cuts so that the saw will do what you want it to do without forcing it. Practice until all you have to do is guide the saw so that it will do the work. To test how well you are doing, take a log and cut thin wafers off the end of it. You should be able to make wafers thin enough, but with an even thickness throughout, that you can see light through them. A good man can make wafers that are nearly paper thin. If you can't, then your saw is not correctly filed, or you haven't yet learned to control it, or both.

Kinesthesia

If you are a normal human being, you can close your eyes and still touch the tip of your nose with your finger on the first try. This ability to know where your body parts are without seeing them is called the kinesthetic sense. It develops in a child as he grows and exercises. Certain special exercises, such as some of the isometrics, are designed to specifically help the kinesthetic sense.

Extending this sense to include objects held in the hand, specifically, to the chain saw, you should know where the tip of the chain saw bar is at all times without looking at it because in many instances it can't even be seen (for example, when the bar is buried in a log). You must practice until you "know" where the cutting bar is, just as surely as a baseball player knows where his bat is at any point in time and can connect with a thrown baseball without having to watch the movement of the bat.

Unfortunately, a person's kinesthetic sense varies with certain conditions. Kinesthesia resides in both the conscious and subconscious levels of the brain. Consequently, certain stresses can affect it. The sense of awkwardness that descends upon a person when he is embarrassed is due to a loss of the kinesthetic sense that allows him proper control of the movements of his body. Consequently, a cutter who is nervous, fatigued, or apprehensive about the situation he is working in loses to some degree his kinesthetic sense—when the logger can't see the tip of the cutting bar and doesn't know where it is by kinesthetic sense, then he's in trouble. Therefore, some methods of cutting seem better than others because they depend less upon the kinesthetic sense. In addition, however, the beginning cutter should work to physically condition himself and to practice as much as possible with his saw in order to develop his kinesthesia to as high a level as is possible.

CHAPTER 4

Felling

Anyone can fell a tree. The mark of a professional logger is that the tree ends up on the ground where the logger wants it. If you "hang up" a tree—that is, get the tree you are felling to fall into another tree instead of all the way to the ground—or fell the tree into a position where it is hard for a skidder to get it out, you ruin your crew's production; and, of course, if you fell it on your head or on a co-worker's head, you or he could be seriously injured or killed.

Felling Theory

The theory behind proper felling is very simple but often overlooked. The idea is this: Never cut all the way through a tree; instead, leave a small strip of uncut wood that will bend like a hinge and guide the tree to the ground in the proper location. If you cut through that hinge, or if your cuts are not planned correctly so that the hinge is broken as the tree starts to fall, then you have no control over the tree whatsoever. *Everything you do in felling must be directed towards creating and maintaining that uncut strip of hinge wood in exactly the right location.*

Getting Ready

Before cutting any tree, check all the conditions that might affect what happens to it. The first thing to look for is defects in

THINK OF THE UNCUT WOOD AS A HINGE!

Fig. 46—Felling cuts are made in the way they are in order to provide a hinge made of the wood fibers that are left uncut. This hinge will guide the tree to the ground at the desired spot.

the tree. Actually, you shouldn't even walk in the woods without glancing up from time to time to make sure there are no "widow-makers" (dead limbs or rotten tops) that might break off and fall on you. These widowmakers can fall because of wind, because of the vibration caused when the saw cuts the tree, or because they are struck by a tree that is falling, even though the tree that they fall from is untouched by your saw. Therefore, look not only for the defect in the tree you are going to fell but also for defects in the other trees around. Also, look for any signs of butt rot. Any hollows, cankers, rotten areas, or fungi are clues that there is unsound wood. Such wood will not do as hinge wood, and the tree may break off when you cut only part way through.

Next, decide which way the tree should go. Working with the skidder operator, decide upon a location in which the skidder can easily hook onto the tree on the ground and haul it out.

After deciding which way the tree should go, look for lean. Trees don't grow straight. Generally, they lean toward one direction or another. Whether or not the tree leans in the direction you want it to go and how badly it leans can make a big difference as to the method of cutting you use. If you stand at the base of the tree and look towards the top, you will probably have a hard time determining which way it's leaning. It is easier if you take a

WATCH OUT FOR THESE...

LEAN   UNEVEN BRANCHING   ICE & SNOW

Fig. 47—(Left) A tree that truly has lean; that is, the trunk of the tree is not vertical. (Middle) The trunk is vertical, but the tree will want to fall in a certain direction because of the heavier branching on one side. (Right) Ice and snow build-up can cause the tree to be heavier on one side.

couple steps back, look at the top of the tree, and then glance straight down at the ground. Now, are you glancing at the base of the tree or to one side? In other words, try to find the vertical line first and then compare the tree to it.

Next, look at the balance of the tree. Even though a tree may lean in the direction you want it to go, it may have more branches on the opposite side. In northern winters, you may find much more snow and ice on the north side of the tree than on the south side, or you may find that the tree may be more shaded by trees on one side than on the other, or that there may be other trees that are closer and rub the snow off one side. After looking the whole tree over, decide which way its weight will want it to go.

Check which way the wind is blowing. Is it going to help you put the tree where you want it or is it going to hinder you from putting the tree that way? A crosswind may blow the tree sideways off its mark. Actually, a good man can use a slight gusty wind to help throw the tree into the wind, but only if he knows which way the wind is blowing. Make sure *you* know!

What about the place where you are going to fell the tree? What does it look like? It should be flat and clear. If it has a big

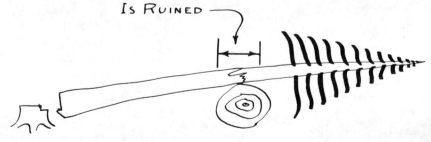

Fig. 48—You must fell the tree in such a way that it will not be damaged. The shattering of fibers within the tree reduces the value of the wood.

hollow in it, it may cause a timber break, that is, the fibers within the trunk may break, thus lowering their grade. If there's a hill or the trunk of another tree strikes it, the trunk may rebound high in the air and strike you or knock some other tree down which will strike you. Small saplings that may become bent over by the fallen tree will make "springpoles," that is, small trees or limbs which are in tension and are just waiting to strike you when you cut them. Plan your felling job so that the tree will end up in a clear, flat area and, if necessary, cut any small trees in the way.

Finally, clear out a good retreat path for yourself. When the tree starts to go, you want to leave just in case something should go wrong. If the tree strikes something on its way down, it may very well kick off the stump and jump back, opposite to the direction in which you expected to fell it. Therefore, your retreat path shouldn't be directly opposite where you are felling the tree but rather it should be about 45 degrees from that.

Now that you have looked the tree over and know that it is absolutely "perfect" (most trees, of course, seldom are)—it doesn't have any lean, it doesn't have any defects, it is perfectly balanced, its diameter is less than the length of the bar of your saw—and now that you know in which direction it will fall and have your retreat path all laid out, you may attack the "perfect" tree.

Felling the "Perfect" Tree

Remember, you're going to have to cut into the tree from both sides, leaving a straight strip of sound, uncut wood to act as a hinge. As a tree falls one way, the cut on that side of the tree will tend to close up; and, as soon as it does, the force of the tree falling will break the hinge right off, and you will no longer have any control. So, you have to cut away the wood on one side of the tree up to the hinge and leave a wide enough space so that the cut won't close.

Generally, cutting away a wedge-shaped piece with about a 45-degree angle will be sufficient. This will guide the tree until it's about 45 degrees off vertical before the hinge breaks, and by then, the tree is almost totally committed to going the right way. Larger wedges can be cut, although generally they are not necessary. For example, a wedge with about a 90-degree angle will guide the tree all the way to the ground if the tree is growing in a level area. With the smaller wedge, the tree breaks the hinge off

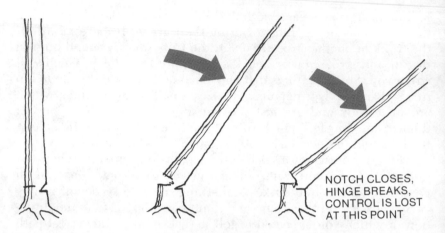

Fig. 49—As soon as the cut closes up on the falling side, the hinge breaks, and you will have no more control. Generally, the tree should fall about 45 degrees before the hinge breaks.

by itself shortly before it reaches the ground. With the larger wedge, the hinge remains unbroken when the tree reaches the ground. This is not desirable, for the hinge will have to be cut, and cutting the hinge fibers which are under a great deal of stress could pinch the saw and thus take away from production time. Furthermore, the larger the wedge that is taken out in the under-cut, the more fiber that is wasted off the butt log.

On the other hand, if the undercut is made less than 45 degrees, the tree will not be guided long enough. You should be sure that the tree is definitely committed and has momentum in the right direction before the hinge wood breaks.

When making the undercut, you must make two cuts. Although it doesn't matter which you make first, the most popular method is to make the horizontal cut first, and since the tree should fall at 90 degrees to the hinge wood, you can fairly accurately determine which way the tree will go by imagining a line at right angles to the cutting bar that is making the cut. Then make the second cut from the top down at a 45-degree angle, meeting precisely with the other cut in order to remove the wedge-shaped piece of wood. However, if one of the cuts extends past the other one, then, in fact, the hinge wood is partly severed. In making the back cut, you could easily overlook the extra cutting you made by mistake on the undercut and cut the hinge wood right off. If this were to happen, the tree may very well fall backwards or to one side or the other, at the very least ending up in the wrong place, probably damaging your saw, and possibly hurting you.

Furthermore, the two cuts should come together in a straight

HOW TO CUT OFF A CORNER...
...WITHOUT EVEN KNOWING IT

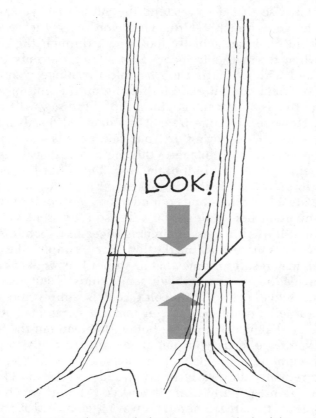

LOOK!

Fig. 50—A common mistake. Instead of meeting, one or both of the cuts necessary to make the notch went past each other. If the hinge is cut through on one side only, it is called "cutting off a corner." This may well result in a tree falling to one side instead of down its intended line of fall.

line, or if not that, the intersection of the two cuts should form a curve line that bows outward at the ends. The "corners" of the hinge wood are what really guide the tree. If the intersection of the two cuts forms a convex line, bowing outward in the middle, the hinge wood will be broken off early, and the tree will not fall straight outward but will fall toward one side or the other.

Students in the Scandinavian logging schools are taught to make the first cut down from the top at a very steep angle. There are three advantages to this method. First, it results in a very open notch so that the tree will be guided close to the ground before the hinge wood breaks. Second, as the cut becomes more nearly vertical, the saw is cutting into the hinge wood less than if it was going in horizontally, so that if you extend the cut too far, you will not harm the hinge as much. Third, when you make the second or horizontal cut, you can actually look down through the first cut and see when the two cuts meet. This allows the cuts to meet precisely and without cutting too far into the hinge wood. Also, the block of wood cut out ends up resting on the cutting bar. In small wood this is an advantage, for a flip of the saw will remove the block. However, in large trees it is a decided disadvantage to have this heavy block sitting on your saw because it can pinch your saw. Another disadvantage to this method is that it results in greater fiber loss from the butt of the tree. This fiber loss is not as important in pulpwood as it is in saw timber.

There are a few other kinds of undercuts, most of them archaic and not important here unless you still use a crosscut saw. One, however, is still used in certain circumstances in which it is desirable to have a square butt on the log. For example, the square butt, which may result in somewhat less fiber loss, is necessary for the proper feeding of logs through some kinds of automatic mill machinery. Actually, the "Humboldt" cut is simply the normal undercut turned upside down. You make a horizontal cut first, then come up diagonally from the bottom to clean out the notch.

After you have made your undercut, you are ready to put the tree on the ground. First, take a quick look around. You should have your retreat path clearly in mind and see that nothing will prevent you from speedily using it, and you should watch out for other people in the area. There is always a chance that someone might walk unknowingly into your area or that the skidder could be coming back for its next load. When you are satisfied that the area is clear, you are ready to go. The back cut is made above the

UNDERCUTS

REGULAR

HUMBOLDT

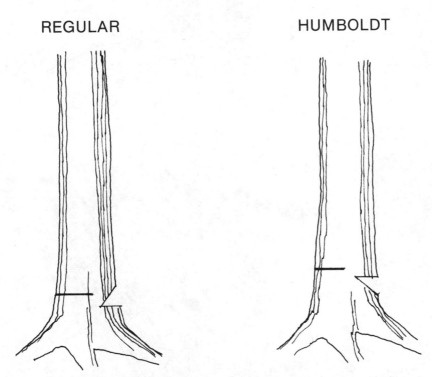

Fig. 51—A variation of the usual form of undercut is to make the notch upside down. In order for the log to pass through certain mechanized machinery, and on very large trees, this may be necessary to save some fiber.

level of the line where the two cuts that formed the undercut came together. For small saw timber trees, it should be at least 2 inches; whereas, on large trees, it may be much more. This is necessary to protect against the tree kicking back off the stump as it falls and, also, to help prevent fiber damage. Furthermore, you generally want to leave nearly an inch of hinge wood on small trees, and, of course, much more (about one-seventh of the diameter is about right) on large trees.

Now you can visualize where the back cut will end on the side of the tree nearest you. Place the bumper spikes of the saw right there. Rev the saw up, and, with it pivoting on the spikes, let

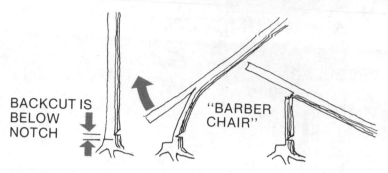

Fig. 52—Placing the back cut above the notch will reduce the tendency to split or "barber chair."

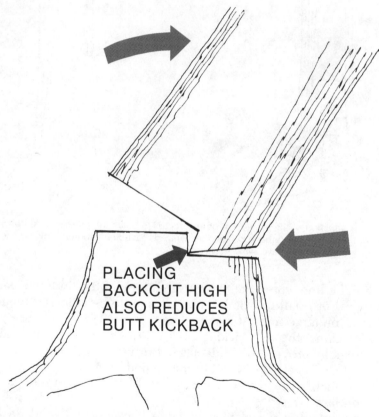

Fig. 53—Even after the hinge has broken, the two pieces of the tree are caught on one another in such a way that the tree is less likely to slide back off the stump, if the back cut is above the hinge.

the chain start cutting into the wood. When the bar is far enough into the tree to enable you to put a wedge behind it, do so. Release the throttle, stick a wedge in, and give it a smack with the heel of your hand. (You're not trying to wedge the tree down at this point—you just don't want the wedge to fall out.) Check again that the cut on your side of the tree is going to end up where it is supposed to. If not, you will want to reposition the saw and get another grip with the bumper spikes to make sure the cut will end up properly. Continue to cut and, as you do so, stretch around so that you can see where the cut should end up on the far side of the tree. Watch the bar and, when the saw has cut up to that point, stop. Take the saw out of the tree, shut it off, and place it in a safe place.

By this time the tree may already have started to fall. You will know this when there is a sharp cracking noise, when the saw bar begins to look loose in the kerf, or when the wedge you put in starts to tilt downward and becomes loose. If you are leaning your body against the tree during the cutting process, which you should be in order to conserve your strength, you will feel the tree as it starts to go, both by its movement and also by a change in vibration as the fibers in the tree start to break. If you notice any of these signs, take the saw out and retreat.

But it may be, if this a perfectly balanced tree, that it has not fallen when you have cut up to the hinge wood. Don't make the mistake of trying to cut more hinge wood. If the hinge is already the right dimension, and you cut any more, you will lose the control of the tree that you had. Instead, put the saw in a safe place, take your second wedge, place it in the kerf alongside the first, and hit the two wedges alternately with an ax or hammer. Again, the same signs as before will tell you when the tree starts to fall. When it does, retreat carefully along your escape route. Retreating carefully, of course, does not mean turning your back on the tree and running. It means calmly keeping your eyes on what is happening and backing away. Be especially alert for branches being knocked down, not only out of the top of the tree being felled but also from others nearby. Even when the tree is on the ground, there is still a danger from objects in the air, so don't rush right back. Wait a few moments to make sure that anything that is going to fall has done so.

Why those two wedges? Well, if you had stuck just one wedge in the tree, it might have bounced out of the cut when you hit it

A COMMON ERROR

THIS HINGE HAS **NO** STRENGTH . . .

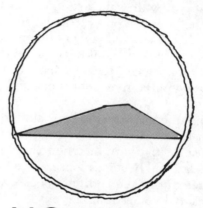

THERE IS **NO** CONTROL OVER THE DIRECTION THE TREE IS TO FALL.

Fig. 54—Another common mistake. If you make the back cut this way, you may find that the hinge is very strong and that the tree won't fall, so you keep cutting until you have cut off both corners as is shown here. Consequently, you will have no control over the direction the tree will fall. You can do the same thing while you are cutting a notch, with the result being that the hinge will break too soon, and you will again lose control of the tree.

(particularly in hardwoods and especially in the winter). If that had happened, you would have been out of business since the kerf would have closed up and there would be no place in which to put a new wedge. Sometimes with an ax you can chip away a "V-shaped" notch along the edges of the kerf and get a wedge started there again, but it's not easy. It is better to put two wedges in and then if one kicks back out you still have the other to keep the kerf open while you put the first wedge back in. Driving them alternately keeps them both tight enough so that if one kicks out the other will hold.

The method just described for making the back cut is the one that you should certainly start with. Often you will see men cut in with the top of the bar up to the hinge on the far side and then,

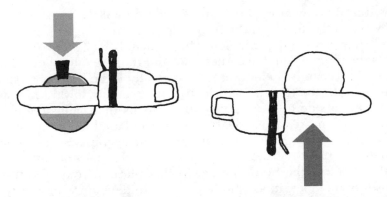

Fig. 55—The steps in cutting a tree with a diameter of less than the length of the guide bar.

TO DRIVE A WEDGE IN DEEPER...

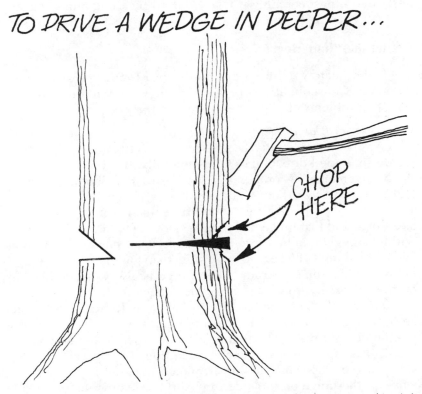

CHOP HERE

Fig. 56—Sometimes it's necessary to drive a wedge in very deeply. You can drive it in deeper if you chip some of the tree away. This wastes some wood fiber, but it is much safer than some of the other methods used to get a tree down.

pivoting the saw around the tip, cut the rest of the back cut until they reach the hinge on the near side. It is true that you probably don't have to stretch as much. Unfortunately, it is also true that many men often "cut the corner off," and the tree falls over toward them. Fortunately, in most cases, especially if the logger has some contact with the tree, he will realize it is coming toward him and step to one side to avoid injury. But this method helps the chain saw dealers make a great deal of money on handlebars, clutch casings, and starter housings that they sell as replacement parts. When you pivot the saw around the tip of the bar, the only thing that is holding the tip of the bar in that place is your kinesthetic sense. Remember, it takes long practice to develop your ability to that point. Remember, too, that under certain stress your kinesthetic sense is lessened. It therefore seems safer to use the method described—most certainly it is to be used by a beginning logger.

Felling the "Imperfect" Tree

Unfortunately, all trees are not perfect trees. Perhaps none of them are. Consequently, you need to know how to deal with the specific problems of "imperfect" trees.

Trees with a side lean: Instead of leaning in the direction in which you want it to fall, the tree may in fact lean at a right angle to your intended direction of fall. Generally, this problem can easily be overcome by proper application of the "holding corner" technique and by proper wedging. You will remember when you were cutting the perfect tree, you left an uncut strip of wood to act as a hinge and that hinge had parallel sides. That is, it was an even width throughout. On a tree with a side lean, however, you must make the hinge thicker on one side than on the other. This is known as "holding a corner." The hinge is always made heaviest on the side *away* from the lean. This is because that side is under tension, and if it is made too thin the hinge will break on that side and allow the tree to fall in the direction it is leaning. Of course, you don't want the total amount of hinge wood to be too great for there to be too much resistance to falling, so you can cut away some of the wood on the side in which the tree is leaning. The wood in the hinge on the side opposite the lean is under tension, that is, it's trying to be pulled apart, so you want to leave it thick. The wood on the hinge on the side that has the lean is under

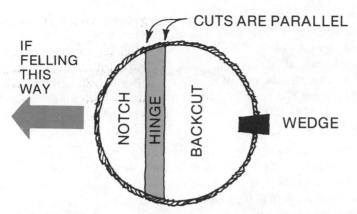

CUTS ARE PARALLEL

IF FELLING THIS WAY

NOTCH HINGE BACKCUT

WEDGE

Fig. 57—In looking down upon a tree that does not lean, you can see that the back cut and notch are made parallel so that the hinge is an even thickness throughout and that the wedge is in the center of the back cut.

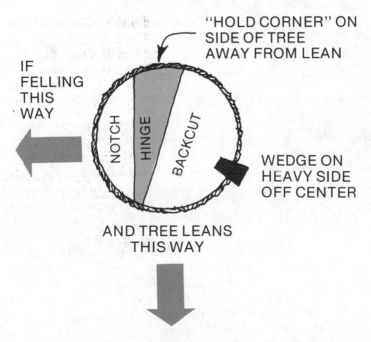

"HOLD CORNER" ON SIDE OF TREE AWAY FROM LEAN

IF FELLING THIS WAY

NOTCH HINGE BACKCUT

WEDGE ON HEAVY SIDE OFF CENTER

AND TREE LEANS THIS WAY

Fig. 58—When the tree leans to one side, the normal hinge may not be strong enough and may break; thus you will lose control of the tree. In this case, "hold the corner," that is, leave the hinge thick on the side that is under tension (on the side of the tree away from the lean).

compression. It doesn't matter if you cut some of it off since the two pieces will simply be pushed together anyway. Don't make a mistake and hold the wrong corner, for the tree will certainly break off and fall the wrong way. Similarly, when you place your wedges, you should not place them in the center of the back cut, but rather you should place them away from the center toward the direction that the tree is leaning. This helps to hold up the tree from falling that way.

Trees that lean away from the way that you want them to fall: Sometimes a tree leans north, and you want to fell it south. If the lean is very much, you must do things backwards. If you were to make the undercut first, you wouldn't get very far into the back cut before the tree would pinch the saw in the cut. So, simply start with the back cut. When you start cutting, place the wedges as soon as possible, finish cutting up to where the hinge should be, and take the saw out. Then, cut the notch from the front, put the saw away, and start wedging. Be sure to leave the hinge thick enough because it will be under a great deal of strain during this process. In fact, the wedges may not have enough lift nor enough strength to get the job done. It may be necessary to cut out a pocket with the nose of the chain saw bar, place an automotive hydraulic jack in, and jack the tree over. (It helps to put a steel plate on top the jack to keep it from digging in.)

Trees with a heavy forward lean: Certainly, you would like the tree to lean in the direction in which you want it to go. But, in fact, if the tree leans too far in that direction, it may cause problems. What can happen is that, before a back cut can be completed up to where you would like the hinge to be, the tree starts falling because of the tremendous weight trying to bend it in that direction. So, the tree starts to move when the hinge is much too thick, too thick to be bent. As a result, the tree "barber chairs" or splits up the middle. This split is generally parallel and in back of the hinge and continues up the tree, slowly moving toward the outside. This split may continue up the tree many feet before the tree eventually finds a weak spot and breaks at that point. The result is that the tree pivots high up on the barber chair and the butt of the tree moves violently backwards. Loggers have lost their lives this way. All trees will do this, but it is especially prevalent among hardwoods, of which oak seems to be one of the worst. But even a

HINTS FOR LEANING TREES...

IF A TREE LEANS THIS WAY...

AND YOU WANT IT TO FALL THIS WAY

① ②

CUT BACKCUT FIRST; PLACE WEDGE; CUT NOTCH; THEN DRIVE WEDGE.

TO FALL IN THE DIRECTION OF A HEAVY LEAN:

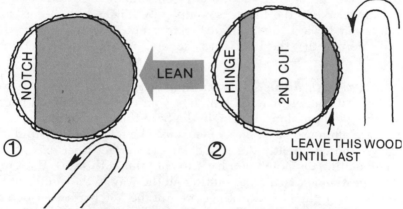

NOTCH

LEAN

HINGE

2ND CUT

①

②

LEAVE THIS WOOD UNTIL LAST

CUT NOTCH; PLUNGE CUT FROM SIDE LEAVING HINGE AND BACK WOOD; THEN CUT BACK WOOD FROM OUTSIDE.

THESE METHODS ELIMINATE BUTT SPLITTING— THAT MEANS MORE SAFETY & BETTER SCALE FOR YOU!

Fig. 59—If the tree wants to fall in one direction and you want it to fall in another, cut the back cut first before you weaken the tree by cutting the notch. Then place your wedge, cut the notch, and then wedge the tree over. Although it would seem easy to fell the tree in the direction in which it is leaning, in the case of a heavy lean, that's not necessarily so. When making the back cut in a tree with a heavy lean, plunge cut, cut up to the hinge, and then cut back out of the tree. By leaving a thin strip of wood on the back side of the tree until last, you can keep the tree from falling until the hinge is the proper thickness.

small amount of butt split will degrade a good saw-log butt into pulpwood.

Since the problem is caused by the hinge being too thick to bend when the tree falls, it is easy to correct the problem by doing two things: First, you want to saw a thin hinge, and second, you want to hold the tree until that hinge is ready. The proper method is to make the undercut first, somewhat smaller than usual. Then, take the saw and plunge in at right angles to the notch and cut out the center of the tree. Make sure that the hinge wood is good on both corners. Sometimes, if there is a great deal of butt swell, it helps to make small "splint cuts" on both sides of the tree to square off the corners, but don't overdo it. This can help to prevent splinter pole from the outside at the corners of the hinge wood. Now, start to make the back cut, but don't cut the wood at the back of the tree. Instead, plunge cut into the tree and cut up to the hinge. When the hinge is completely finished, then cut backwards out toward the back of the tree until the tree falls. Also, make certain that the back cut is several inches above the undercut.

Trees with diameter larger than bar length: Finding a tree larger in diameter than the length of your cutting bar is not necessarily a great problem. In fact, in the Scandinavian countries, small bars are often used as a safety measure. The technique is similar to the technique already described for the perfect tree, except that when cutting the notch you have to cut from both sides. If there is any question about the bar cutting all the way to the center of the tree, make a plunge cut in the center of the notch as described for trees with a heavy forward lean. Then, plunge cut on what will be the far side of the tree, cut up to the hinge on that side, and then start walking around the tree, cutting as you go, towards what will be the near side of the tree. As you pass the halfway point, remember to stop and put in wedges.

Snags: Dead and diseased trees, often called "snags" or "stubs," are a major cause of death in the woods. You must be very careful when working around them or with them. Wood that has deteriorated will not form hinge wood because it will not bend. It will simply break off. If you have any question about cutting a tree which appears to have some sort of defect, get the advice of an experienced logger. Large trees that have obvious defects should be downed either by winch or by dynamite.

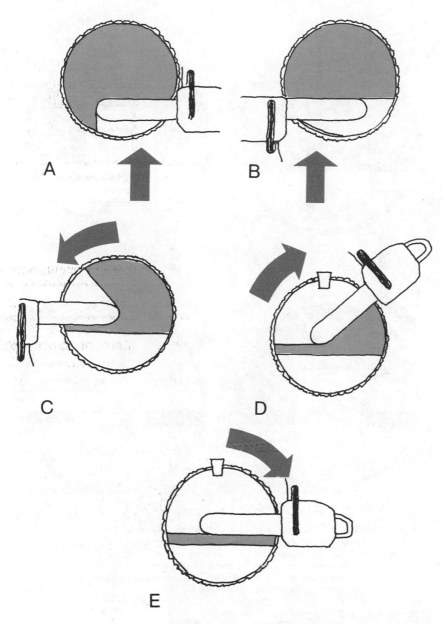

Fig. 60—The steps in cutting a tree with a diameter less than twice the length of the guide bar.

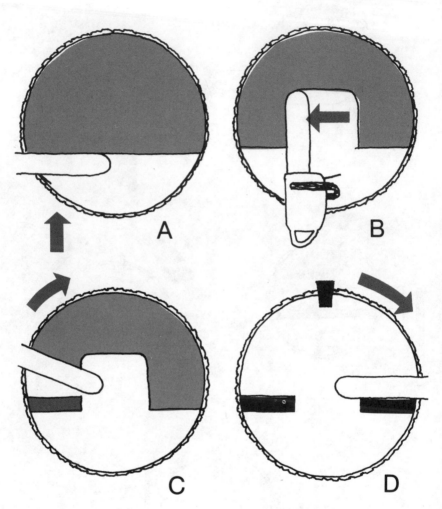

Fig. 61—The steps in cutting a tree with a diameter somewhat greater than twice the length of the guide bar. When making a back cut, plunge cut, cut up to the hinge, and then walk around the tree. If you hold the saw as shown here with the chain turning in this direction, you will lessen the risk of kickback. You can achieve even greater safety by switching hands on the saw so that the left hand operates the throttle and the right hand is on the front handlebar, placed on that portion of the bar which is normally on top when the chain is upright. With the saw held in this way, the chain brake probably will function if there is a kickback.

74-S-17

ACCIDENT IN SPITE OF CHAIN BRAKE

BACKGROUND: A man in Massachusetts was felling pine with a popular make and model of a Scandinavian chain saw. This saw was in perfect condition and was fitted with a chain brake and safety chain.

PERSONAL CHARACTERISTICS: The man, while not presently engaged as a logger, was felling trees on the weekend. He was considered to be a skilled, careful worker and had had no previous accidents or injuries. He was not, however, wearing safety equipment at the time.

UNSAFE ACT OR CONDITION: The man was felling a white pine that measured approximately 22 inches on the butt end. The saw had a 16-inch bar. Therefore, as the man started the felling cut, his hand was not in a position to trip the safety chain brake, and the nose of the bar was buried in the tree.

ACCIDENT: The saw kicked back out of the cut and struck the man in the left upper thigh.

NATURE OF INJURY: The logger was cut crosswise in the upper left thigh. Fifty internal stitches and 22 surface stitches had to be taken. It is estimated that he will lose from 14 to 21 days of work.

Fig. 62—This kind of cutting on larger trees can result in serious injury due to kickback of the saw when the tip of the bar touches uncut wood, as attested to by this report of just such an accident—even though this saw had a chain brake. Most chain brakes will not work when the saw is held in the felling position.

Widowmakers: You are reminded again that limbs, dead or otherwise, that may break off are a serious danger in the woods. These limbs can be either on the tree which you are felling or on another tree and can be brushed off by the tree you fell. Obvious widowmakers should be treated exactly the same as snags. At the very least, trees near widowmakers should be felled by an experienced man, with an observer stationed at a safe distance to warn him. But, a tractor with a winch may do the job better. Remember, too, that it takes a long time for many branches to fall to the ground. Often they ricochet around and get caught and teeter for awhile before falling. In one case a man was injured by a limb which had broken off the pine he was felling and had fallen into a small maple tree which threw it back up in the air like a sling shot. The branch came down some time later to injure the logger. So, whenever you fell a tree, wait a few moments and then look and listen before you approach the downed tree.

Other personnel in area: Again, too, you are reminded that every year many men are injured by trees felled on them. Keep a sharp eye for outsiders wandering into your area. If you have any questions whatever as to whether or not an outsider knows he is in danger, stop cutting and don't continue cutting until he leaves. When you are cutting, no man should be closer to you than twice the height of the tree you are felling.

Rough ground: Rough ground causes problems of its own. A tree fallen across some other object will kick up at the butt and may injure you. And, while a small hardwood tree may fall on practically anything and not be damaged, a large softwood will break to pieces on anything less than a flat surface. Indeed, some pine is so soft that it will shatter upon striking a foreign object, just the same as a pumpkin thrown onto the ground—thus, the name "pumpkin pine." Obviously, wood so damaged is degraded seriously. As a matter of fact, some pieces may be broken up to where they are not even suitable for pulp. It is said that in the days of "masting," that is, when the large old growth pine were cut for the masts of sailing ships, men worked for days to cut all the small trees and stumps and smooth the earth where one of the great pines was to fall. While such drastic measures are not usually necessary today, you should be aware of the problem in order to get the most money for your labor. Never fell a tree over a rock outcropping, boulder, or other downed tree. Never fell a tree across a hollow in the ground, such as a small valley carved by a brook. Likewise, never fell a tree downhill, but rather try to send it diagonally up the hill. A few minutes spent in planning the fall of a large tree will be amply rewarded.

Hangers: A tree doesn't always go where you want it to, and sometimes it will get caught or hang up in another tree. There are many different methods which were used in the past to get these trees to the ground—and most of these methods are well documented in logging companies' accident files. The safest way is to get a tractor.

Lower limbs: Some trees have limbs all the way to the ground. With some spruce trees, for example, you have to cut your way in before you can find the tree. The proper technique is to hold your saw in front of you at shoulder level or lower and perpendicular to your body (in a position so that you are able to read the trademark on the bar). This way you can move up to the branches and cut them off from the front of the tree, so if the saw kicks, it will kick off to the side and away from you. Once you have cut a hole in front of you, you can place the bar on the other side of the tree but still perpendicular to you and cut off the other limbs as you walk around the tree. Don't be lazy here—cut them all off. You want to be able to work without being constricted, and especially if something goes wrong, you want to be able to get out of there.

Butt swell: In some trees the diameter of the trunk increases very rapidly in the last few feet above the ground. With a large, high-value tree, it may be necessary to make a series of cuts around the tree with one cut vertical and the other horizontal to trim the size down. Then you can proceed with felling the tree normally. This is necessary because the debarking equipment at some mills may not be able to handle the rapid taper, thus, throwing the log out of the machine and endangering the mill operator. You could trim the tree up after it's on the ground, but you will probably find that if it's that swell-butted your bar won't be long enough to handle it anyway, so you might as well do it before the felling.

Small trees: At times you will have to fell small trees (and perhaps against a lean) that are so small that there is not enough room to get a wedge in behind the bar. You may also want to use the breaker bar or Swedish felling lever, a tool very much like a hardened steel crowbar which is used instead of a wedge. If you use this, you don't want it in the same kerf as you are cutting in,

Fig. 63—The log breaker, which is very popular in Sweden, is commonly used on small trees instead of wedges. Note the hook which unfolds and converts the tool into a kind of peavey.

because if you should move the saw back and strike the felling lever by mistake, your chain will certainly be ruined. In this instance, use the "three-quarter cut." After making the normal undercut, go to the far side of the tree and make three-quarters of the felling cut by cutting right up to the hinge from that side, but hold the saw engine out away from the tree so that you do not make the far side of the felling cut. Then, insert the wedge or felling lever and come back to the near side of the tree. A tree, of course, is composed of fibers running lengthwise, and as long as those fibers are cut at some place, the tree will fall down, even though they aren't cut in the same place. You will now finish off the back cut by making a cut that overlaps the first back cut but slightly lower than it, so that you are not in the same kerf. Actually, the saw is generally tilted so that the outside of the cut appears normal, but in looking at the stump afterwards, you can see where the tip of the bar was down below the first cut. By using

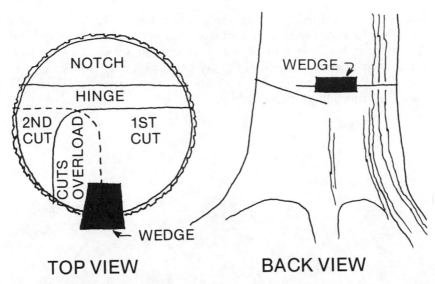

TOP VIEW   **BACK VIEW**

Fig. 64—The three-quarter cut allows you to use a wedge or felling lever or bar on small diameter trees. Make the normal notch. Make the back cut in two steps: When making the first cut, leave some wood uncut on one side of the tree in order to hold the tree from falling. Then, place the wedge or felling lever in this cut. Make the last cut to finish the back cut, but make it lower than the first back cut. This way the saw can't strike the wedge or lever. Make the last cut at an angle below and overlapping the first back cut.

this method, you can't strike the wedges. When you have cut up to the hinge, then use the wedges or breaker bar to fell the tree.

The Swedish felling lever, breaker bar or log breaker, is an excellent tool that is not much used in the United States and probably should be. It will not do for very large trees, but on pulpwood-size trees, it can be faster and is easier to carry around than an ax and wedges. The tool, which looks very much like a small steel wedge welded on the end of a crowbar, is inserted in the cut like a wedge. When you have finished the cutting, you can grasp the end of the bar and lift it to lever the tree over. Most breaker bars have a small step welded on the back part of the wedge, so if lifting the bar up as high as you can is not enough to push the tree all the way over, you can very quickly slip the bar down and into the cut further so that the tree will not be sitting on the little step. This time when you lift the bar, the tree should go the rest of the way over. Occasionally, you will be working in small timber just right for the breaker bar and will encounter a larger tree which is too heavy for you to lever over. You can cut a small sapling as a long pole and use it to pry under the handle of the breaker bar, the end of which is curved in somewhat of an open hook shape. Generally, the tree will go over; if it won't, the bar is still holding the saw kerf open. Then, insert wedges and carry out the normal procedure.

CHAPTER 5

Limbing

In order to ready the tree for market, you must remove the limbs and buck or sever the trunk of the tree into sections of proper length. In products, such as those made from pulpwood, where quality of fiber configuration is not important, you may limb and buck at the same time or even buck first and limb after. However, in an integrated operation, where quality of fiber configuration is important, you must study the trunk of the tree in order to decide what products to obtain and, hence, where to make the bucking cuts. Consequently, unless the tree is to be bucked for pulpwood or fuel wood only, limbing should always precede bucking.

In limbing large hardwoods, you actually "buck" off the limbs. Of course, you may limb softwoods in the same way; however, the regular placement of limbs on softwoods, especially spruce and fir, lends these trees to a more systematized approach.

"Scandinavian" Limbing System

It takes time and practice to master this system for limbing, and until you have done so, it seems awkward. However, once you learn it, you will find the system is fast, productive, less fatiguing, and reportedly safer. There are six positions or "stations" that are repeated in succession as you work from the butt to the top of the tree. These are in order:

1. *Cut on right side with pushing chain.* Begin by standing

6 STEPS IN SWEDISH LIMBING...

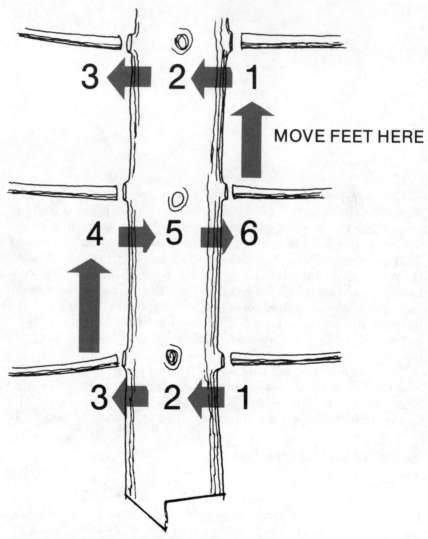

Fig. 65—There are six steps or "stations" in the Scandinavian limbing system. The logger moves along the tree, cutting limbs off both sides and off the top. When these branches are all gone, the tree will generally fall over onto its side, thus allowing the logger to cut easily the branches which were on the bottom.

on the left-hand side of the tree, with your right leg braced against the tree. Pivot the saw on the crankcase of the engine, which is resting on the top of the tree, by pushing down on the rear handlebar. This will cause the cutting bar to raise and the first limb to be cut by the chain on the top of the bar.

2. *Top cut with pushing chain.* Slide the saw across the top of the tree to where the cutting bar is parallel to the ground, and again, pivoting the saw by using the engine casing as a fulcrum, cut the next branch on the node* that is protruding from the top of the trunk (again, with the pushing chain on the top of the cutting bar).

3. *Cut on left side with pulling chain.* Pivot and twist the saw so that it is again upright. By using the clutch casing against the tree as a fulcrum, pivot the saw so that the cutting bar goes down and the pulling chain on the bottom of the bar cuts off the next branch on the node.

4. *Cut on left side with pushing chain.* Slide the saw along the tree to the next node and pivot the saw (still using the clutch casing as a fulcrum) back to a more horizontal position. Doing so moves the cutting bar into the first branch on the next node, cutting it with the pushing chain on the top of the bar.

5. *Top limb with pushing chain.* Slide and twist the saw to where it is lying on top of the tree, with the engine up and the bar horizontal and roughly parallel to the tree. Pivoting the saw on the clutch casing will cause the pushing chain on the top of the bar to cut the next branch in the node. Often it is more comfortable to use your thumb to operate the saw's throttle when in this position.

6. *Cut on right side with pulling chain.* Next, twist and roll the saw on the tree in order to bring it into a position where the saw is upright and the cutting bar is roughly parallel to the tree. Actually, to assume this position, you are rolling the saw on the chain against the tree. "Blipping" the throttle slightly will cause the chain to pull the saw ahead, much like a crawler tractor, and will help to get the saw into position. Then, pivoting the saw on the engine

---

*The "node" is the place on a tree where a group of branches grow.

Fig. 66—At the first station or step in the sequence, position the saw as shown in order to cut a branch on the right-hand side of the tree. The saw is resting with the engine on the top of the log. By pressing down the rear handlebar, you can move the cutting bar upward, cutting the branch with the top side of the bar.

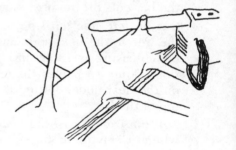

Fig. 67—At the next station, roll the saw over so that again pressure on the rear handlebar toward the tree will rotate the saw about the point where the engine contacts the tree and cut a top branch with the top of the cutting bar.

Fig. 68—Again, roll the saw on the tree and lift on the rear handlebar to force the cutting bar down, cutting a branch on the left side of the tree.

Fig. 69—By sliding the saw ahead slightly
and by pushing down on the rear handlebar so that the saw pivots around the
clutch casing, you can raise the cutting
bar, thus cutting off another branch on
the left-hand side of the tree with the top
part of the cutting bar.

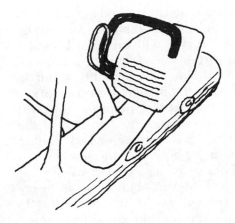

Fig. 70—By rolling the saw on the tree,
you now have the saw in the correct position so that moving the rear handlebar
and again rotating about the clutch casing
will cause the saw to pivot and cut a top
branch with the top part of the cutting
bar.

Fig. 71—Rolling the saw again results in
this position. Raising the rear handlebar
causes the saw to rotate around the engine again, and the bar will move downward and cut a branch on the right-hand
side of the tree. This completes the sixth
station, and without moving the saw from
this position, you can take a step forward
so that your right leg is again braced
against the tree with your left leg slightly
forward, and you are ready to begin
again.

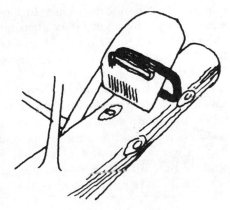

crankcase will let the bar swing down, cutting the last branch in the node with the pulling chain on the bottom of the bar.

While carrying out these six steps, you never support the weight of the saw with your body—the feet do not move, the body remains braced against the tree, and the saw never leaves the tree. After these six steps have been completed, the saw is on the right-hand side of the tree with the bar sticking down. You can let it rest there (still holding on to it, of course) and walk forward a couple of steps and place your feet to be ready to cut the next branches by repeating the same series of six steps. In this way, you are never moving when the chain saw is.

Several other safety factors should be considered here. First of all, cut only the limbs on the top and sides of the tree. Attempting to reach under the tree from the left side will tire your back, for you will be holding the weight of the saw. Attempting to reach under the tree from the right-hand side will probably result in your cutting your legs or feet. Leave the branches on the bottom until all the other limbing is finished. At that point the tree will fall over, and you can walk right down the tree, cutting off the remaining branches (which will all be in a more or less straight line), by using the pulling chain on the bottom of the saw.

Second, avoid kickbacks. These can be avoided by several methods. Above all, watch the tip of the bar. Many times in heavy brush and when limbing spruce you will not be able to see the tip of the bar. You have to know where it is by your kinesthetic sense. A shorter bar will help tremendously, for it is less apt to get down into trouble. And, as mentioned in the section on bar length in Chapter 1, it is not necessary to have a very long bar to fell good-sized trees. However, it is absolutely important that the engine should always be at a very high rpm before the chain starts cutting. This will also reduce the chance of kickback. A good operator keeps the engine rpm up, although he varies the power to meet the demand by varying the throttle setting. A poor logger puts the saw against the limb to be cut and then gives it more power so that when the chain touches the wood it is going slowly. That is not good technique. Remember, as pointed out in Chapter 2, when correctly tuned for the maximum power, the engine is running slightly rich at wide open throttle, and this limits engine rpm to an acceptable maximum. (It also gives maximum power when in the cut.) Repeating from Chapter 2, the chain must be kept filed sharp and to factory specifications, not only for longer chain life but also for less chance of kickback. Of course, your saw should have a chain brake on it, but the chain brake will not work in all positions and at all times, so you must also watch these other factors.

"Sweep" Technique

This technique is used on trees with many small branches. It is faster, of course, but it also involves more danger from kickback. Always be sure of your footing. Never move the saw while you are moving and always be *behind* the saw. Keep the engine at full throttle and sweep the bar back and forth across the tree, cutting the branches off the sides and top—but do *not* sweep on past your own body.

The basic technique and the "sweep" technique can be merged and modified, depending upon the tree being limbed. With a tree that has irregular limbs, for example, it may be necessary to use the first technique, but omit a few of the stations if there aren't any limbs there. As the limbing on trees becomes more and more irregular, then the basic method is used less and less. On large hardwoods, simply walk beside the tree, "bucking" the limbs off as you come to them.

Problems

The main problem is that many of the limbs will be bent under the tree's weight and therefore will be under a great deal of stress. Even limbs under moderate amounts of stress can cause the saw to become bound in the cut. It pays to consider mentally each branch, particularly large branches, and ask yourself what would happen if that branch were cut. Well, obviously the cut on one side would open up more than a cut on the other side because of the stresses placed on the limb. That is the side you want to cut from. If the limb is under a great deal of stress, then when you cut it, it may lash out with tremendous force. Many loggers have been seriously injured by such "springpoles" and "jill pokes." When a branch is under extreme tension, make sure you are clear of it when you cut it and then "nip" the limb on the inside (the side which is being compressed) in order to release some of the tension before you carefully cut through from the side under tension.

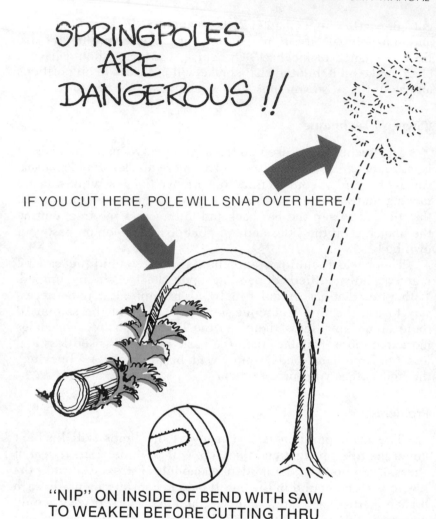

SPRINGPOLES ARE DANGEROUS !!

IF YOU CUT HERE, POLE WILL SNAP OVER HERE

**"NIP" ON INSIDE OF BEND WITH SAW
TO WEAKEN BEFORE CUTTING THRU**

Fig. 72—Watch out for springpoles! If you cut through from the outside, the sapling will suddenly snap straight back and may injure you. Weaken the springpole first by making a couple of small cuts on the inside of the bend.

CHAPTER 6

Bucking

Bucking or severing the trunk of the tree into logs of proper length and quality can have an extremely large effect on the value of the products produced. That means that proper bucking can make you, a professional logger, more money for the same amount of work.

Technique

You must measure the various lengths so that you can make the cuts at the appropriate places. There are several measuring devices which you can use. By far the most common device for saw logs in the Northeast is a pole cut to the proper length. The pole, which is generally 6, 8, or 10 feet long, is marked every 2 feet. If you do use a pole, mark the end with paint, or very carefully, squarely, cut so that if by accident the saw trims an end of the pole the fact that the pole has been damaged will be readily apparent. Countless numbers of logs have been cut to the wrong length because the measuring pole had been damaged.

The measuring pole is sometimes also used for pulpwood. However, the pole is awkward and heavy and has to be carried around. When working with 4-foot pulpwood, you can use a much better method—"whips" that can be attached to your chain saws. These are metal or plastic rods much like a radio antenna on a car. They are clamped to the rear handle of the chain saw and adjusted so that the overall length of the saw with the whip is 4 feet long. This allows the saw itself to be used for measuring the pulpwood.

Fig. 73—A self-rewinding logger's tape with a sharp hook on the end is useful in many types of bucking.

Special logging tapes are also available. They have a hook in one end which is attached to the end of the log. The tape, which is contained in a round box with a spring-loaded pulley attached to your belt, unwinds as you walk down the tree. After you make the cut, pull on the tape, and a hook on the end of the log will release, allowing the tape to rewind into the container. This is an especially good device for long logs, for the tape is light, compact, and easy to handle. However, under no circumstances hook the end of the tape into the butt of the tree and walk all the way down the tree marking out the logs as you go. For one thing, you will probably forget the bucking allowance (which is discussed on page 100), but more importantly, you cannot buck for grade, and you will lose a lot of money this way. Some general specifications of the various products follow.

Bucking Pulpwood

Pulpwood is wood from which the fibers will be chemically or mechanically separated in order to produce pulp and paper. Since the fibers will be eventually separated anyway, their arrangement in the various pulpwood sticks is not very important. In general, you could go right down a tree cutting 4-foot pulpwood by making a cut every 4 feet. A small amount of crook or bend in the log would not make much difference. Of course, a lot of pulp sticks with excessive bend in them make it hard for the trucker to put on a full load, but the specifications for this product are much lower than for saw logs.

In the Northeast, traditionally pulpwood has been generally cut into 4-foot lengths. This is because groundwood "grinder" stones are only 4 feet wide. In the "good old days," most handling was done manually, and a 4-foot length of the size of the trees then available was thought to be the most that a man should handle all day long. Now there is a move toward 8-foot lengths of wood (which can be more efficiently handled with today's machinery) and also toward tree-length wood, which is the most efficient of all to transport to the mill. As in all products, the lengths that you should be bucking depend upon the customer for your wood, and so you should direct any questions about proper bucking to the pulpwood buyer or to the scaler who is more or less the buyer's agent in determining the amount of wood you have cut.

Bucking Saw Logs

Saw logs are to be made into lumber. Lumber varies in grade and hence price, depending upon the arrangement of the fiber within it. The quality of the fiber is also important. While a small defect in pulpwood sticks does not cause great problems at the pulp mill, a small amount of defect in a log can ruin it at the saw mill. In general, the perfect log would be absolutely straight and have no taper and no knots or other defects. This is a general statement because some lumber has a higher value if it does have certain types of knots or other defects, for example, "knotty pine."

Saw logs generally have to be 8 feet or longer, generally in even 2-foot increments. That is, 8-foot logs, 10-foot logs, 12-foot logs, etc. Sometimes hardwoods are accepted in odd foot lengths as well. That is, logs could be cut 8 feet, 9 feet, 10 feet, 11 feet, etc. Often, although not always, lumber is sold in packages of various lengths. When the buyer purchases lumber in such a package, he expects all lengths to be present, and, therefore, would not, for example, accept a whole package of 8-foot boards. You, the logger, are a key man here since it is obvious that the saw mill cannot turn out 16-foot lumber from 8-foot logs. On the other hand, you should not necessarily cut all 16-foot lengths since a 16-foot crooked log may turn out only 8-foot lumber anyway, and with a great deal of waste.

It is almost impossible to cut the logs exactly perpendicular to their axis. Since the bucking cut will not be square, if you attempt to cut a log, say, 10 feet long, then some of the boards will be slightly less, and a board that is 9 feet and 11 inches long must be cut back to 8 feet before it can be marketed. Consequently, loggers always leave a "bucking allowance" on each log. That means a 12-foot log, for example, would actually measure about 12 feet and 3 inches long. This allows for a cut that is not perfectly square (although every attempt should be made to make it so), wood shrinkage as the log dries, and enough extra wood so that the lumber can be trimmed at the mill to be exactly the right length. Again, a small failure here can be very costly since a log exactly 10 feet and 0 inches long will be scaled as though it was an 8-foot log.

Bucking for the highest grade yield out of any given log is an art in itself. Every saw logger should obtain and read the publication, "Felling and Bucking Hardwoods, How to Improve Your Profit," by F. J. Petro, Publication No. 1291, Canadian Forestry Service. Basically, however, the trick is to get as many straight logs as is possible from a given tree, even if you have to waste some of the fiber. Suppose, for example, that a tree has been felled and topped and you now have a tree-length log that is 36 feet and a few inches long. Unfortunately, the trunk has a sharp bend in it, 14 feet from the butt end. The beginning logger (and especially the beginning logger who does not limb the tree nor take a look at it first) walks right up the tree bucking out three 12-foot logs as he goes. When the scaler comes, he will find a good 12-foot butt log, a good 12-foot top log, and a virtually worthless 12-foot log from the middle of the trunk. The experienced logger would have stopped, looked at the whole tree, and made a few cuts that would have resulted in a straight 14-foot butt log, and then straight 12- and 10-foot top logs. Since the quality is much, much higher, he would have been paid much more for making only one more cut. This is not to say that the log should always be cut as long as possible. If that same 36-foot tree had been evenly but strongly curved throughout (called "sweep"), the logger might have been better

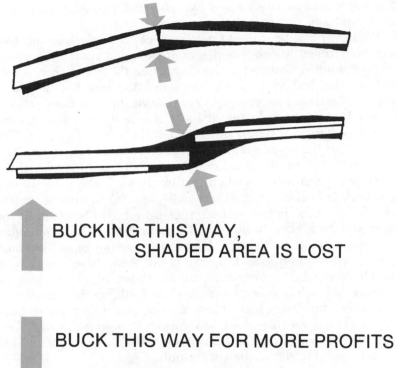

BUCKING THIS WAY,
SHADED AREA IS LOST

BUCK THIS WAY FOR MORE PROFITS

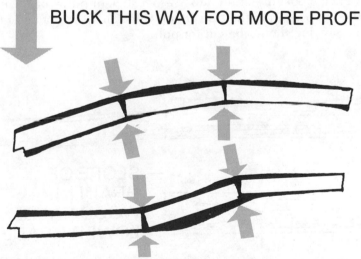

Fig. 74—Two logs, each bucked in two different ways. The top log has "sweep." The bottom log in each case has "crook." Assuming the logs are bucked where the double arrows are, there will be a tremendous amount of wood fiber wasted, as indicated by the black area shown in the top of the illustration.

off to cut it into two 8-foot and two 10-foot logs—each log would have been more nearly straight.

Whatever can be done to get the highest grade logs must be done. Sometimes "blocks" or pieces of wood too short to be of any use are cut out. This is often the case when there is a sharp offset bend in a log (called a "crook") or when the tree is crotched or forked. Oftentimes, loggers try to cut down through the center of the crotch and trim it so that it looks like a straight log. A good scaler, however, will spot it and discount the value of that log. The reason is that the wood grain within that crotched fork bends as it merges with the trunk. Since the slope of the grain is one of the factors taken into account when grading lumber, the value of that log is less. It is also true that the grain standing almost on end in that portion of the board will often cause a board to catch in the planer and be kicked back violently against the planer operator. So, for safety reasons, too, it is best just to cut out blocks containing this part of the tree and discard them. Sometimes people will come to the logging operation to get these blocks to use for firewood, to cut into fancy tables, and so forth, so the fiber is not necessarily completely lost. It may also be possible in some cases to block out a crooked section into a 4-foot stick of pulpwood. Certainly, the top portion of the tree which is too small in diameter to become a saw log should be cut for pulp.

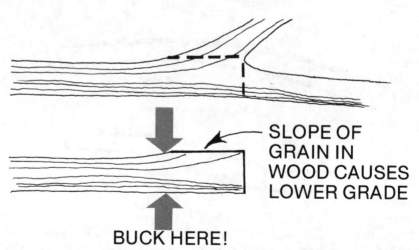

SLOPE OF
GRAIN IN
WOOD CAUSES
LOWER GRADE

BUCK HERE!

Fig. 75—It is usually not desirable to try to trim up a crotch to get a slightly longer log. Because the grain twists and turns at the crotch, boards cut from this piece will have an extreme slope of grain.

Bucking Other Products

There are very many other tree products which can be used, such as boltwood, veneer wood, firewood, log cabin stock, etc. Generally, the specifications for these products depend upon the mill that will buy them. By all means, make sure you explore all the possible markets for wood in your area and integrate your logging operations to get the maximum value from the trees that you have. A short definition of each of these products follows:

Boltwood: Boltwood is wood that is used in turnery mills to be made into certain products. For example, birch can be made into toothpicks, dowels, spools, toys, etc. The turnery mills generally want the wood to be completely free from defects and to be of certain, sometimes unusual, lengths.

Veneer: Veneer logs are logs that are peeled into thin sheets to be used generally for making plywood. The specifications depend upon what grade plywood is used. Obviously, finished plywood to be used for paneling is of extremely high quality indeed. One way of defining a veneer log would be to say that it is an ideally perfect saw log. However, the price paid for veneer is generally greater than for saw logs, and so if you can get together a load of logs of veneer quality, you will make more money by sending them to the veneer mill.

Firewood: At one time, of course, firewood was the most important fuel in the world. Even today over half of the volume of wood used in the world is for fuel. Recently, the demand for firewood in the United States has grown again, and in some areas it has grown very rapidly. But firewood is sold according to local customs. Some people want 12-inch lengths of firewood, some 16-, some 18-, some 24-inch, and some 4-foot. Again, you will have to search out the market in your locality.

Problems

There are a number of problems you will run into when bucking wood.

Binds: If Columbus had been wrong and the earth had been perfectly flat, it would have simplified the task of logging, for when a tree is perfectly straight and lies on a perfectly level surface, you can make the cuts by cutting right down through the tree from the top. However, if the ground is not flat and the log is supported at each end, then if you try to cut down from the top, the kerf will close and pinch the saw. You must either use wedges or, using the top part of the chain (if there is enough room to do so), cut up from the bottom of the log. A log supported so that one end is free and clear has its own problems. In this case, the weight of the log is such that if you cut down from the top, the log will

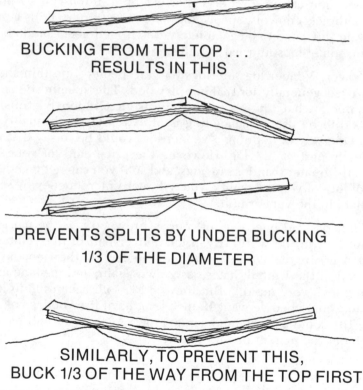

**BUCKING FROM THE TOP . . .
RESULTS IN THIS**

**PREVENTS SPLITS BY UNDER BUCKING
1/3 OF THE DIAMETER**

**SIMILARLY, TO PREVENT THIS,
BUCK 1/3 OF THE WAY FROM THE TOP FIRST**

Fig. 76—If a log is unsupported on one end, and you buck all the way through from the top, the log will split as shown. If you try to buck all the way up from the bottom, when the kerf closes, you will pinch your saw. Therefore, buck up from the bottom about one-third of the way, and then finish bucking from the top. In the same way, a log supported at two places will split if cut all the way from the bottom or will pinch your saw if cut all the way from the top. Consequently, cut one-third of the way from the top and finish bucking from the bottom.

split and break off before you can cut all the way through. So you must cut up from the bottom one-third of the thickness of the log and then make a cut down from the top to finish it off. Remember, a split in the timber will degrade its value.

This technique is also used to prevent splits where a log is supported at each end. In that case, make the cut by cutting a third of the way down from the top and then finish up the cut from below. If instead you make the cut all the way down from the top and use wedges, you will not need to make the one-third-of-the-way cut. However, using wedges takes more time.

When the log does lie flat on the ground, the problem is how to cut it without cutting down into the dirt and ruining your chain. The answer is simply to control your saw well enough that you don't cut all the way through the log but just cut all the way through the wood, leaving a small strip of bark between your chain and the ground. This takes practice, and certainly no more than the bark should be left. Otherwise, when the loader or skidder comes to move the logs, he won't be able to break the logs apart, and you'll have slowed down the rest of the operation. Leaving logs cut only partially through will bring you a not-too-polite discussion with the boss.

Safety factors: There are some safety factors to be aware of too. The first is kickback. This is especially prevalent when bucking 4-foot wood in piles. Often, tree-length wood is brought out and "decked" up in a pile by a skidder. Then, one man bucks down through the tree-length wood, converting it to 4-foot wood in the pile. The chances are extremely high that the tip of the saw blade will touch another stick in the pile and the saw will kick back. Again, you must develop the kinesthetic feel for where the tip of the saw is, keep your eyes open, and by all means, use a chain brake and other protective gear.

Springpoles, as mentioned in Chapter 5, may also be present here. Oftentimes, small saplings get bent under the tree as it falls and may be released when the tree is bucked. Look for them, cut them partially from the inside to release the strain, and finish cutting them carefully from the outside before you buck the log.

By the way, the first bucking cut you will make is to "top" the tree. This means cut off that portion of the tree which is too small to be merchantable. Most loggers do this as they complete the limbing. They simply slash across the top of the tree, cutting with the top of the bar, and pulling the saw towards them. This is a neat, quick way of doing it, but it may also neatly and quickly cut your knee. Take another half step, turn the saw back horizontally, and cut, using the pulling chain and the bottom of the bar. It is much safer and the few extra seconds required may save you many months in the hospital.

Large logs that may roll on slopes are also a danger. Whenever possible, you should be on the uphill side of the log when you are bucking it. If you can't do this, then block the log firmly with stones or small blocks cut from limbs to keep the log from rolling before you commence bucking.

You must still keep one eye peeled for other personnel in the area. In this case you're not worried just about a log that will roll down and hurt someone else—you also must be careful that *you* don't get hurt by other people and equipment in the area. Watch that someone doesn't drop a tree on you while you're limbing and bucking. Be especially watchful when skidders move by—many men have been hurt when a log being pulled by a skidder hit an obstacle and was thrown sideways, slamming against a logger working in the area.

CHAPTER 7

The Cutter as Part of
a Logging System

The logger is not one man alone on the earth. He exists as part of a large group of people that includes the landowner, the forester, the skidder operator, the trucker, the wood procurement man, and ultimately the customer for the paper, lumber, toothpicks, veneer, plastics, and all the other products that are made from trees. To be a useful and productive member of the system, the logger must understand his place in it. Therefore, a short description of the process of turning trees into final products is necessary.

The landowner may be an industrial forest company, the collective public through the administration of the U.S. Forest Service or various other governmental agencies, or some other group, but more increasingly he is a private person who owns a few acres of land. Close to cities where taxes are high, it may well be costing him more to own the land and pay taxes on it than he would get in return from the wood cut from it. So, why does he own it? Probably because he wants to own a piece of forest. This may mean that someone has gone to a great deal of trouble to convince him that proper forest management is the correct thing to do and that the forest will remain healthy and productive after it has been logged. By a few careless mistakes, of course, the logger can convince the landowner otherwise—he can in fact convince that forest owner, as well as all the other landowners who see or hear about such land, that the forest is ruined by loggers who cause endless erosion and other forms of destruction and that logging should be prohibited. Certainly it costs a little bit more to do a good job, to not damage the reproduction any more than is absolutely necessary, to water bar roads to prevent erosion; but in the long run, it's a cheap investment in the availability of future stumpage.

The forester is the logger's friend. His job is to keep the forest productive and to determine which trees should be cut. He is trained in knowing the needs of the various species of trees and in prescribing what harvesting system is appropriate. Some forests should be selectively cut so that the oldest and largest trees are taken out, leaving the younger trees to grow. This is done because some trees must grow in the shade of other trees. The forester may mark each tree that is to be cut; or sometimes, he uses the diameter-limit system in which trees of a certain size and larger are to be taken and may be either marked or left for the logger to measure.

Some trees cannot tolerate shade as well as others and must have lots of sunlight to grow properly. Generally, for these species, the forester uses even-aged management in which the trees are all of one age. That is, they all started to grow at about the same time when the old trees were removed. Usually, this is by means of a clear cut in which all trees of all sizes are removed and new trees are planted or seeded. In the seed tree method, a few mature trees are left to provide a natural seed source for the area. In the shelterwood system, a large percentage of the trees are cut, but some are left to provide protection for the younger trees starting out. When the young reproduction is firmly established, then the remaining mature trees are cut. Even-aged systems are often also used for species like spruce which usually grow in wet areas and are not windfirm. If the selection system was used in these areas, the removal of one tree might cause many other trees nearby to blow down and that wood would all be lost. Since the problems of *silviculture* (the science of growing trees), erosion control, insect and fire protection, and other subjects are so complex, a professional forester must prescribe the proper methods for each forest.

Unfortunately, many loggers regard the forester as an ivory tower thinker who is trying to prevent the logger from making a good living. Actually, it is just the opposite. In the long run, the forester's expertise will provide more trees for the loggers to cut in the future. It is true that some beginning foresters do not understand the complexities of logging, but it is equally true that many loggers have an inflated, erroneous impression of their own knowledge of forestry. The solution is for loggers and foresters to talk and work together for the mutual good of both and the eventual benefit of all citizens.

On large operations, the logger may have only one job to do. On small operations, he may have to be an all-around logger who is able to perform the tasks of the right-of-way crew, the cutter, the skidder operator, the bucker, the scaler, and the trucker. In order to understand the system better and to have more job opportunities, the logger should at least know something about each task and at best know how to perform several.

The right-of-way crew clears and pioneers roads into a cutting area. Its job is to make sure that the logs that are produced can be transported to the market place. Quite often, crew members are loggers from other areas assigned to this job temporarily.

The cutter (faller, feller, chopper, saw hand, or whatever local term is in use) fells, limbs, and often bucks the trees into the merchantable products. His job is not only to convert the trees into logs but also to place the logs so that they can be easily extracted from the woods. Because his actions determine log quality and ease of log extraction, no man has as much effect on the productivity and profitability of a logging crew as the cutter does. If the cutter's productivity suffers, the productivity of the whole system suffers. The cutter who works like a mad man and outproduces the skidder may make it harder for the skidder to extract each log, thus increasing logging costs.

And it may well be that that same cutter will injure himself. Then his production will go down, and every phase of the system will lose productivity. For example, the cutter has a kickback and cuts himself in the leg. Immediately his own production ceases. The skidder operator also has to stop work, come in and give the cutter first aid. While he's doing that, he isn't bringing out any logs for the truck driver to carry, so the driver's productivity suffers. Furthermore, the foreman who has been trying to keep all operations going efficiently has to stop and drive the cutter out in his pickup truck. Not only did the productivity suffer, so that men were not bringing any money into the system, but also money continued to go out of the system. The cost and finance charges of the skidder probably run around $10.00 per operating hour. The skidder must be paid for regardless of whether it is bringing out any

THINK OF THE MAN ON THE SKIDDER!!

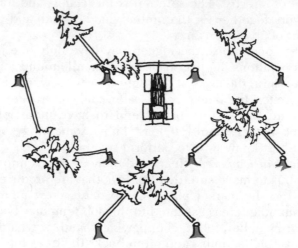

HELPING HIM HELPS YOU MAKE MORE PROFIT

Fig. 77—Timber should always be felled so that it can be easily removed from the forest. (Top) Notice that the locations of the tree stumps are identical. (Bottom) The trees here have been felled so that the skidder operator may easily hook onto them and pull them out of the forest.

logs. The same is true of the log truck, loader, and so forth. Again, the cutter is the man most important to the efficiency of the entire operation—when his production ceases, so also does that of the entire system.

The skidder operator moves the wood from the stump out to the "landing" where it will be loaded onto a truck for movement to the market. The skidder operator's task is influenced to a large degree by the method in which the cutter drops the logs. If they are in a neat herringbone pattern so that the skidder operator can easily hook onto the logs and skid them down the skid trails to the landing, then he can move a great deal of wood in a relatively short time. If the logs are crosswise to the skid trails, he will have to spend a great deal of time juggling them out from around stumps and other trees. Or, if the trees have all been downed on top of one another in a great big jackstraw of logs, then his productivity will suffer.

Both the skidder operator and the cutter have a responsibility to protect reproduction in the area as much as possible. Those young trees that are driven over, those trees in the remaining stand that have been barked and girdled by having logs skidded against them, will not grow to be trees of a size that a logger can cut to make his livelihood.

The bucker converts the trees into the proper lengths (if the trees are bucked at the landing). He has a very large effect on the dollar value of those trees. A few cuts in the wrong places can convert good wood into products with only a fraction of its potential value.

The loader loads the bucked logs onto the truck for transport. With the smaller trucks, most of which are self-loading, the loader operator will probably be the truck driver. On large operations, a mobile crane is used to load the various trucks, and the loader is operated by one full-time man.

The scaler measures and in some cases determines the grade of the products which the loggers have produced. Scaling may be done in the woods or at the mill. Sometimes it is done by a weight scale; oftentimes it is done with a specially graduated measuring stick. The scaler has the right to subtract from the scale shown by the stick or weight scale for various forms of defects in accordance with product specifications.

And, of course, *the trucker* delivers the logs that the loggers have produced to the mills where many other people will manufacture the products used by thousands of people. But the productivity of this whole chain of people, as well as the availability of wood due to landowners' desires and government laws and regulations, depends in a large part on the logger's actions.

Logging Systems

Various types of logging systems are used today. A few of these are as follows.

Shortwood systems: Logs are bucked to a certain specified length. This is sometimes done at the stump and the wood if in log length brought out by a skidder or if in short pulpwood lengths by some sort of a forwarder (a machine similar to a skidder but with a rack in the back to hold the wood) or by a small pickup truck converted for off-road use or by a trailer or sled behind a crawler or wheel tractor. Most operations producing shortwood have found it more efficient to bring the wood out in tree length behind a skidder and then to buck the wood on the landing to the proper length. Not only is skidding more efficient from handling the longer length wood, but it's also easier to integrate the operation on the landing by bucking out the highest possible value products from the wood that comes from the stump.

Tree-length systems: Since it is more efficient to handle one long log once than to handle a number of small pieces, tree-length, long-length, or multiple-stick operations are generally much more efficient and are therefore becoming much more popular. Even though most logs now come from the stump tree length and are bucked on the landing, in some operations tree-length or long-length wood is loaded right on trailer trucks or even railroad cars and hauled directly to the mill for further bucking or processing.

Mechanized Operations

Although "mechanization" means different things in different parts of the country, in this instance it means an operation which uses large equipment instead of individual loggers who use chain saws. This does not necessarily mean that the loggers are being replaced but rather that different tools are being used. For example, the "feller-buncher" is a large machine, often like the hydraulic excavator that contractors use, with shears like giant scissors that snip off trees at the stump and with clamps to hold onto the tree as it shears it. The feller-buncher lifts the sheared tree and places it in a pike or "bunch." Another large machine is the "de-limber" which strips the branches off the log. The "forwarder" is generally a very large skidder with a loader on the back. The loader picks up the individual trees and places them in a special "bunk" or holder which won't let the trees slip when the forward-er pulls them. When the forwarder has a large bunch of trees held in the bunk, it drags them all to the landing. There are also multi-purpose machines available that perform the various tasks of the feller-buncher, the delimber, and the forwarder with just one machine. Some of the machines used in the South are used to pro-duce shortwood; whereas, in most cases, the machines used in the North are used to produce tree-length wood. Although most of these machines are used in the production of pulpwood only, for the shears damage the wood fiber in the butt of the tree and de-grade it for use as lumber, there are experimental machines now being built that have saws or cutting augers to reduce butt dam-age.

Chipping: Many pulp mills use processes in which the pulpwood is chipped before being chemically treated to make paper. Lately, the thought has been, since the wood is going to be chipped anyway, why wait to get it to the mill before it is chipped? The first chippers that were not at the paper mills were located in various saw mills. They chipped the slab wood and other residues which were formerly burned and made them into valuable paper chips which were then trucked to the paper mills. Recently, this line of reasoning has been expanded to include in-the-woods chipping operations in which mobile chipper units, generally mounted on semi-trailers, are moved right into the woods. Generally, softwood trees have to be limbed and debarked because the softwood bark is detrimental to the paper process. However, whole hardwood trees are often chipped right in the woods, and thus the amount of fiber obtained from each tree is greater since the wood in the limbs also is made into paper. How-ever, leaves, twigs and grit embedded in the trees during skidding present processing problems at the pulp mill.

So far, the kind of terrain and the species of tree have restricted the use of these various types of mechanized operations. Therefore, there is plenty of opportunity ahead for the conventional logger, especially in cutting in rough or swampy terrain and in cutting high-quality wood.

CHAPTER 8

Medical Help After Injuries*

Although no one wants any logger to be injured in the woods, injuries do occur, and your knowing a few basics of first aid could greatly assist an injured logger—it might even prevent his death.

The Occupational Safety and Health Act (OSHA) requires that one man in each logging area be trained in first aid. However, it is highly advisable for *every* logger to have first aid training. Such courses are provided by the Red Cross, Civil Defense, Heart Association, Emergency Medical Services, and other organizations, and sponsored for loggers by the American Pulpwood Association, forestry associations, state agencies, and others. Since these courses are extensively available, every logger should take a first aid course as the opportunity arises. Of course, it is beyond the scope of this book to provide a first aid course. However, there are some basics that everyone should know.

The first thing to do after any accident is to make sure that the injured person's air passage is open and that the person is breathing. The unconscious person's tongue tends to fall back and block the air passage (it is, however, impossible for him to swallow the tongue). When a person has stopped breathing, usually all you have to do is open up the air passage, and he'll start breathing again all by himself. A simple maneuver called the "head tilt" will in most cases open his air passage. Do this by lifting the neck with one hand, while pushing down on the forehead with the other to

---

*Prepared in consultation with Maine's Emergency Medical Services Project, Medical Care Development, Inc., Augusta, Maine.

tilt the head back. If the person doesn't start breathing, then give him mouth-to-mouth resuscitation.

After you have the person's head tilted back so that his air passage is open, you are ready to perform mouth-to-mouth resuscitation—simply pinch the patient's nose shut with one hand while placing your other hand under the patient's neck. Place your mouth over his and blow in a deep breath, while you are watching for the chest to rise. Then, take your mouth away and let the patient breathe out, while you are catching a breath yourself. If you put your ear up to the patient's mouth, you will be able to hear him exhale and you will know that your efforts have been success-

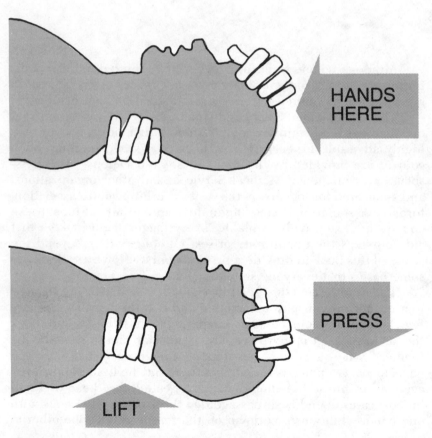

Fig. 78—Tilting the head back, as explained in the text, opens the victim's throat so that he can breathe.

ful. Repeat the process about 12 times a minute. If the air is not going in or out, check to make sure that nothing is blocking his air passage. Normal breathing may eventually start up again on its own, but if it doesn't, you must keep breathing for the victim until you can get him to medical help or until help arrives at the scene.

The next thing to check for is bleeding. Severe bleeding looks terrible and is a great panic producer, but generally it is easy to cope with if you know how. First of all, do not use a tourniquet unless absolutely necessary. Almost all bleeding, no matter how bad, can be stopped simply by putting direct pressure on the wound with your hand, combined with elevating the extremity above the heart if possible. The wound is already contaminated by whatever it was that caused the wound in the first place, so don't waste time running around hunting for sterile dressings or sterilizing handkerchiefs over campfires. Just use your hand.

Occasionally, it helps to use a pressure point to stop bleeding. But this method is not as reliable as direct pressure and elevation. There is nothing mystical about pressure points. They are where the arteries that are carrying the blood from the heart to various parts of the body run along bones in certain places in the body. If you press in those places, you will trap the artery between your hand and the bone and you will squeeze it shut. Remember this rule: Wherever an artery passes over a bone, you can feel a pulse (try finding your own pressure points). Also remember that direct pressure and elevation will solve most of the bleeding problems which you may encounter.

Broken bones, of course, are common in logging accidents. Moving the patient without knowing what you're doing can cause additional injury. There is always the chance, one which you should *never* forget, that if the victim has an injury to the spine (backbone or neck) then *any* movement might paralyze him for life. Consequently, if a man is hurt, for example, a tree falls on him, don't rush right over and drag him out. First *check his breathing*, then stop his bleeding, and keep him safe until help comes.

One of the worst killers is shock. Shock occurs not only from physical injury such as loss of blood but also from the psychological stress involved. To treat for shock, try to maintain the patient's body temperature by using a blanket or your own coat, and, if it's very cold, by getting down with the victim so your body heat can help warm him. Above all, keep him reassured, by talking to him calmly, assuring him that help is on its way and that he should remain calm.

You should also know how to deal with other problems that you may encounter in the woods. One is heat exhaustion and/or sun stroke. Most authorities now agree that salt tablets are not necessary for a normal person who eats a well-balanced diet. However, if you don't feel well in hot weather, there are two things you should do: Don't continue to push yourself if you don't feel well, and consult a physican. The actual treatments for people who develop heat exhaustion and/or sun stroke are well covered in first aid courses, and since it is not a common occurrence in the woods, there is no reason for further discussion here.

The opposite of hot weather problems is, of course, frostbite. Obviously, the best thing to do for frostbite is to prevent it in the first place by being properly dressed. On the other hand, it's possible for a person under severe weather conditions (low temperature and high wind) to get a nose or ear frostbitten very quickly without knowing what's happening. Do *not* rub snow on it; instead, take the victim to a warm, not *hot* place and thaw him out. Do *not* give him any alcoholic beverages. Most important, get him medical attention.

You are not a physician, nor are you to act as one. Your job is to help get the victim to proper medical attention as soon as possible—and still have him in good condition when he gets there.

621.93   Sarna, R
Sarna

          Chain saw manual
REEDSBURG PUBLIC LIBRARY
    345 VINE STREET
  REEDSBURG, WI 53959